KRISTEN C. ECCLESTON, ED. D.

The Perspective Pivot

Stop the Spiral:The Brain Based Tool for Overthinkers, High-Achievers, AND Burned-Out Brains

Contents

Introduction

THE THREE-SECOND REVOLUTION

The hotel room clock read 11:47 PM.

In nine hours, I would walk back onto the set of The Blox, Wes Bergmann's national reality competition show for entrepreneurs, where startups from across the country compete in a week-long intensive boot camp to prove they have the best business on the block.

Just twelve hours earlier, I'd been wearing one of the coveted red jerseys, signaling I was one of the top three entrepreneurs currently in the lead. Then everything fell apart.

One disastrous challenge sent me plummeting off the leader board entirely. When Wes announced the top three entrepreneurs at the end of the day and my name wasn't called, I went from the highest high to the lowest of lows, suddenly sure that my earlier success was just a fluke. The cameras had captured every second of my visible panic. Tomorrow, I'd have to walk back onto that set knowing that everyone had watched me unravel under pressure.

Because nothing says "thriving entrepreneur" quite like publicly imploding on national television.

My spiral voice—that catastrophic inner narrator—was delivering its most vicious performance yet: *You peaked too soon. Everyone's about to watch you fail spectacularly. This will define you forever.*

Two years earlier, before I'd learned what I'm about to teach you, that voice would have won. It would have kept me awake all night, rehearsing every possible disaster until exhaustion dragged me into fitful sleep. I would have walked onto that set the next morning already defeated by my own mind.

But something was different now.

I did something that took exactly three seconds and changed the trajectory of not just that competition, but my entire relationship with pressure, doubt, and the catastrophic voice that had been hijacking me for decades.

I used what I now call The Perspective Pivot.

The next morning, I walked back onto the set and won. Not just that day, but again and again, until I finished as second runner-up in Season 5. A year later, I returned for Season 10 and won. Ultimately, I performed so well that Wes invited me back as a judge for Seasons 20, 22, and 23.

I accomplished all this not because I'd eliminated fear or self-doubt, but because I'd learned to navigate them without letting them run my life.

THE PROMISE

This book teaches you one thing: how to claim the three seconds between what happens to you and how you respond.

Three seconds doesn't sound like much. But in brain time, it's the difference between being hijacked and being free.

In those three seconds lives everything you've been searching for: the ability to stop catastrophic thinking before it hijacks your day, the power to make clear decisions when anxiety screams at you to panic, and the freedom to act from wisdom instead of fear.

But here's what no one tells you about those three seconds: you can't access them until you understand why your brain keeps fighting you in the first place.

That's the missing piece. That's why positive affirmations didn't work. Why meditation apps helped when you were already calm, but disappeared when you actually needed them. Why you can read every self-help book on the shelf and still lie awake at 3 AM catastrophizing about an email you sent six hours ago.

Your brain is doing exactly what evolution designed it to do: scan for threats, prioritize negative information, and prepare you for worst-case scenarios. The problem? It's running 200,000-year-old survival software in a world that doesn't need it.

You don't need to fix your brain. You need to understand it. And then you need a tool that works with your wiring, not against it.

The Perspective Pivot is that tool.

By the time you finish this book, you'll have:

- A three-step framework that interrupts spiraling in real-time
- A physical anchor(hand gestures) that works when cognitive tools fail
- An understanding of the neuroscience that explains why your brain spirals so you can finally stop taking it personally
- A 30-day practice protocol that makes the technique automatic
- Proof that you are far more capable than your anxious mind has ever admitted

You won't eliminate anxiety. You'll transform your relationship with it.

And here's the truth that changes everything: hope isn't dangerous. Your nervous system just learned to treat it that way. This book teaches your brain a different story.

WHY I KNOW THIS WORKS

December 2019. I stood in a small conference room adjacent to my principal's office at the high school where I served as Director of a special education program. That morning, we were managing multiple simultaneous crises: a staff scandal, a psychiatric emergency upstairs. I was providing an update to my principal when my staff sent word: the student at the center of the scandal had just walked through our doors.

Since the scandal broke, I'd been driving to their house every Friday to provide direct instruction. I wanted them to know they still mattered. The realization that they'd come back, that the connection had held, hit like a physical blow.

Gratitude collided with exhaustion. Relief collided with grief. Pride collided with the knowledge that I'd been sacrificing my own well-being to create this one moment of success.

My nervous system looked at all those colliding emotions and declared: Hard stop. We're done.

My vision tunneled. My heart slammed against my ribs. Heat crawled up my neck despite the frigid conference room. I bit my lip, silently begging my body: *Don't faint. They can't see you weak.*

My muscles gave out anyway. I fell forward onto the conference table and began to sob. Undone in front of the very people who counted on me to hold everything together.

That collapse was the culmination of years of ignored spirals, catastrophic thinking I'd pushed through rather than addressed, activation I'd medicated rather than regulated, a nervous system I'd overridden until it finally overrode me.

What followed was several years of intensive recovery. Therapy. Eye Movement Desensitization and Reprocessing (EMDR). Psychiatric support. Completing my doctorate while on medical leave.Leaving teaching permanently. Founding a consulting business. And slowly, painstakingly, developing what would become The Perspective Pivot.

There's a moment in recovery no one warns you about. It's when you realize the person you've been trying to get back to doesn't exist anymore. For me, it came in the middle of a quiet afternoon when everything felt too heavy to carry. My body was exhausted, my mind was foggy, and my spirit felt hollow. I had spent months pretending it was just stress, that if I could power through one more crisis, I'd find my way back to normal. But normal was gone.

The woman who ran a district program for students in crisis while finishing a doctorate, caring for her sick mother, and showing up like everything was fine had reached her limit. I had built my identity around being capable, dependable, and composed, and suddenly I couldn't even fake it.

Grieving that identity was harder than the burnout itself. I didn't just lose my energy. I lost my sense of self.

For so long, my worth had been tied to what I could produce, fix, and hold together. I thought resilience meant pushing through no matter what, but I started to see it for what it was: survival mode that had gone on too long. My nervous system was done. My body stopped negotiating with my ambition. And in that forced stillness, I had to face the truth that the version of me who could carry it all wasn't coming back.

What followed wasn't a quick rebuild or a motivational comeback. It was grief, and then slowly, grace. I began letting go of the parts of me that were built on over extension and guilt. I learned to stop performing strength and started practicing honesty. I stopped asking how to get back to who I was and started asking who I was meant to become. Because healing isn't about finding your old self again. It's about finally meeting the version of you that burnout tried to bury but couldn't destroy.

By August 2022, nearly three years after that conference room collapse, I was ready to test whether I'd actually transformed. I applied to compete on The Blox Season 5.

You already know how that story begins: me in a hotel room at 11:47 PM, spiral voice vicious, having just fallen off the leader board. But you also know how it ends: I walked back onto that set and won.

The difference between December 2019 and August 2022 wasn't that I'd eliminated pressure, self-doubt, or catastrophic thinking. I'd learned to navigate them without letting them destroy me. The spiral voice that once kept me awake all night now lasted three seconds before I could interrupt it.

The woman who collapsed sobbing onto a conference table became the woman who could perform under national television pressure, fall off a leader board, and pivot herself back to victory in three seconds.

That's not resilience you're born with. That's resilience you build, one three-second window at a time.

WHY THIS MATTERS RIGHT NOW

We are living through a period of relentless uncertainty. Economic pressures, technological disruption, political division, and a 24-hour news cycle that never lets the nervous system fully rest — these aren't temporary conditions. They are the texture of modern life. Most people are not burned out because they are weak. They are burned out because they have been living for years in a state of chronic alert, bracing for the next disruption before the last one has fully landed.

That is why this work matters. Learning to pivot your perspective is no longer just a mindset skill. It is a survival skill.

Right now, millions of people are trapped in mental prisons of their own making. They're lying awake at 3 AM, replaying conversations from hours or years ago. They're avoiding opportunities because their minds have convinced them that uncertainty equals danger. They're shrinking their lives to accommodate catastrophic stories their brains create about ambiguous situations.

Think about your own experience:

You lie in bed at night while your mind churns through hypothetical conversations and imagined failures;

You've avoided opportunities because your brain convinced you the risk of embarrassment was too high;

You've spent enormous energy managing anxiety about uncertainty instead of engaging productively with actual challenges;

A vague email from your boss can hijack your entire evening;

One critical comment can erase twenty pieces of positive feedback;

Sunday nights fill you with dread about the week ahead.

This pattern cuts across all demographics because catastrophic thinking stems not from individual weakness but from human wiring attempting to navigate a world it wasn't designed for.

I've worked with:

- CEOs who make million-dollar decisions by day but spiral for hours over a single critical email

- Surgeons who execute complex operations flawlessly but catastrophize about what an attending physician meant by "interesting approach"
- Artists and musicians who captivate audiences but spend hours dissecting every social media comment for hidden criticism
- Teachers who guide struggling students to breakthroughs but convince themselves that one administrator observation will expose them as incompetent
- Parents who research every parenting decision but still lie awake, convinced they're ruining their children
- Students who excel academically while quietly drowning in the certainty that they'll be exposed as frauds

The spiral trap doesn't discriminate.

WHAT MAKES THIS DIFFERENT

You've likely tried other solutions:

Positive thinking worked for five minutes until your next spiral proved that forcing optimism over evolutionary biology doesn't work.

Meditation apps helped when you were already calm but disappeared mid-spiral when your thinking brain went offline.

Atomic Habits taught you habit formation, but catastrophic thinking hijacks you before habit loops can engage.

The 5 Second Rule breaks action paralysis, but doesn't address thought paralysis.

CBT thought records work after reflection is possible, not during emotional flooding.

Manifestation practices helped you set intentions and visualize success, but nobody explained why your brain kept sabotaging you or how to regulate your nervous system so those practices could actually work.

Here's what these approaches share: they either require conditions you don't have mid-spiral, or they fight your nervous system instead of working with it.

And here's what almost no one talks about: you didn't fail at manifestation because you weren't positive enough. You struggled because your nervous system was in survival mode, and your brain's Reticular Activating System (RAS) was filtering for threats, not opportunities.

The Perspective Pivot doesn't fight your biology. It works with it — in three seconds, anywhere, without anyone knowing you're using it.

WHAT YOU'LL LEARN

This book is organized into four parts:

Part I: The Problem

You'll understand why your brain defaults to catastrophe, what's actually happening in your nervous system during spirals, and why your struggles aren't character flaws but predictable biology. You'll stop fighting your brain and start understanding it.

Part II: The Solution

You'll learn the complete Perspective Pivot framework: Acknowledge, Adjust, Align. You'll master the Triple-A Hand Hack (three physical gestures that anchor each step so the technique works even when your thinking brain goes offline). You'll get the toolkit: specific adjustment strategies and alignment actions for real-world scenarios.

Part III: Making It Last

You'll discover how to make pivoting automatic through progressive practice, how to adapt the technique if your brain works differently, what to do when life delivers genuine crises, how to use the Pivot in professional settings, and how to build what I call "spiral immunity" so triggers lose their power over time.

Part IV: Moving Forward

You'll get your roadmap for long-term mastery, including what transformation actually looks like (not perfection, but skilled navigation), when to seek additional support, and how your personal sovereignty prepares you for collective contribution.

* * *

The 30-Day Challenge

This book includes a structured 30-day practice protocol that transforms the Perspective Pivot from a technique you remember to use into a response that happens automatically when you need it.

- Week 1: Foundation practice in calm states
- Week 2: Application to low-stakes frustrations
- Week 3: Integration into genuinely challenging situations
- Week 4: Mastery through high-stakes implementation

Readers who want additional support can access free practice resources at drkristeneccleston.com/the-perspective-pivot

You'll find tools to help you build your PerspectivePivot practice and track your progress throughout the 30-day challenge.

WHO THIS IS FOR

This book is for anyone who's done everything "right" and still feels like they're falling apart.

You might be:

- The leader making high-stakes decisions while secretly convinced you're one mistake away from being exposed
- The parent lying awake replaying every interaction, certain you're failing your child/ren
- The professional who looks composed externally but battles constant self-doubt within
- The creative producing brilliant work while fighting the certainty that you're a fraud
- The student who is excelling academically while quietly drowning in anxiety
- The person who's always felt like their brain is running different software than everyone else's
- The high-achiever who's just now learning that ADHD, autism, or another form of neurodivergence explains why "simple" things have always felt impossible
- The manifestation follower who feels like a failure because staying positive didn't prevent everything from falling apart

You don't need to be in crisis to benefit from this work. You just need to be human in an increasingly overwhelming world, tired of your own mind working against you.

And if you've ever felt invisible (like the world sees your performance but not your pain, like you're holding it together on the outside while falling apart on the inside), this book sees you. All of you. The capable and the struggling. The strong and the scared. The high-functioning and the barely hanging on.

Because here's what I know: the people who look the most together are often the ones spiraling the hardest. You don't have to perform strength anymore. You just need to understand your brain.

IF YOUR BRAIN WORKS DIFFERENTLY

If you have ADHD, autism, or another form of neurodivergence (or if you've always suspected your brain operates on different software than everyone else's) this book was built with you in mind from the foundation up.

Maybe you:

- Know exactly what you need to do but feel physically unable to start (that's executive function, not laziness)
- Experience neutral social cues as devastating rejection (that's Rejection Sensitive Dysphoria or RSD, not you being 'too sensitive')
- Need external structure because your brain won't hold information internally (that's working memory differences, not incompetence)
- Struggle with time perception, where four hours feels like twenty minutes, or you can't track how long you've been spiraling (that's time blindness, not carelessness)
- Process information through movement, visuals, or sound instead of abstract thinking (that's your wiring, not a deficit)

You're not broken. Your brain just needs different approaches.

Here's what you need to know: The Perspective Pivot doesn't just "accommodate" neurodivergent brains. It was designed for how brains like ours actually work, which makes it more effective for everyone.

Throughout this book, you'll find specific adaptations woven into every chapter, not as afterthoughts, but as core methodology. You'll learn how to externalize what your working memory can't hold, how to shrink actions when executive function won't cooperate, how to regulate sensory overwhelm before attempting cognitive tools, and how to build automaticity on your timeline, not someone else's.

And if you don't know yet whether you're neurodivergent, that's okay too. Use what resonates. Your brain knows what it needs better than any label.

As of 2025, research from the Centers for Disease Control and Prevention (CDC) and the World Health Organization (WHO) estimates that approximately 1 in 36 children and 1 in 45 adults are on the autism spectrum.

Roughly 5 to 7 percent of adults worldwide meet criteria for ADHD, though many remain undiagnosed until adulthood, particularly women and high-achieving professionals whose compensatory strategies often mask core symptoms.

Recent studies also reveal that over 80 percent of neurodivergent adults report experiencing significant anxiety, burnout, or emotional dysregulation connected to masking, executive dysfunction, or chronic self-doubt. Research by Hudson et al. (2019) found that autistic individuals are four times more likely to experience clinical depression over their lifetime compared to neurotypical peers. Cassidy et al. (2018) found that autistic adults show approximately four times higher rates of suicidal ideation and three times higher rates of suicidal attempts than non-autistic peers.

These findings underscore why nervous system regulation, executive function scaffolding, and self-understanding are not luxuries. They're essential. The Perspective Pivot was designed with this reality in mind: to help every brain access calm, clarity, and confidence without having to fight against its own wiring.

THE REVOLUTION STARTS NOW

The space between stimulus and response, between what happens to you and how you respond, that is your freedom.

Viktor Frankl discovered this principle while surviving Nazi concentration camps. He understood that external circumstances can constrain your choices, but they cannot eliminate your fundamental power to choose your response.

This power exists in every moment, waiting to be claimed.

In that space between trigger and reaction, everything becomes possible. You can feel rejected and still maintain your self-worth. You can face criticism and extract valuable information without accepting character assassination. You can encounter uncertainty and remain curious rather than catastrophic.

The Perspective Pivot teaches you to expand that space from milliseconds to seconds, creating room for choice where none existed before.

You don't need to "raise your vibration." You need to reclaim your regulation.

Your next spiral isn't evidence of failure. It's an opportunity to practice.

Your next moment of uncertainty isn't a crisis to avoid. It's a chance to build evidence that you can navigate the unknown skillfully.

The revolution starts now. Not when you feel ready. Not when the fear goes away. Not when you've read every chapter and memorized every technique.

Now. With your next three seconds.

Because right now, as you finish this introduction and turn to Chapter One, you have a choice. You can let your spiral voice tell you this won't work for you, that your anxiety is too severe, that you're too busy, or that nothing will ever help.

Or you can decide that the next time you notice catastrophic thinking hijacking your mind, you'll claim the three-second space between trigger and spiral.

You won't do it perfectly. You'll forget sometimes.

You'll spiral anyway.

And that's exactly as it should be, because this isn't about perfection. It's about building a skill that transforms your relationship with your own mind, one imperfect practice at a time.

In that three-second space lies everything you've been searching for: peace with uncertainty, confidence in challenge, and the unshakeable knowledge that you are more capable than your spiral voice will ever admit.

The space is already there, waiting between every trigger and every response.

The only question is: will you claim it?

Welcome to the revolution.

I

THE PROBLEM

1

The Spiral Trap

"The cave you fear to enter holds the treasure you seek."
— Joseph Campbell

Your brain doesn't spiral because you're weak. It spirals because it's trying to protect you.

That voice in your head catastrophizing about the vague email from your boss? That's your nervous system doing exactly what evolution designed it to do: predict threats and keep you safe. The problem isn't that you overthink. The problem is that your brain thinks overthinking equals preparation, that if you imagine every worst-case scenario, you'll somehow be ready when disaster strikes.

You won't. You'll just be exhausted.

Here's what's actually happening when you spiral: your brain is running an outdated threat detection program designed for physical danger (predators, environmental hazards, social rejection that could get you cast out of the tribe) in a modern world where most threats are psychological and imagined.

Throughout this book, you'll meet several people whose spirals will feel familiar. Marcus, Sarah, Jamie, Elena, and others are composite characters drawn from nearly two decades of my work — my time as a special educator, my work as a coach, and conversations with workshop participants across the country. All identifying details have been changed. You may see yourself in more than one of them.

The calendar invite appeared in Marcus's inbox on Monday morning at 10:17 AM.

Subject: Check-In When: Tuesday, 2:00 PM From: Manager Note: None

Within sixty seconds, his pulse had spiked. His stomach dropped. The spreadsheet in front of him blurred as his mind raced: *What did I do wrong?*

Marcus, 38, was a financial analyst at a mid-sized investment firm. Solid track record. Good relationships with his team. Consistent positive reviews. The kind of employee who arrived early, delivered ahead of deadlines, never caused drama.

Which made what happened next all the more exhausting.

For the next twenty-eight hours, Marcus's brain hijacked him completely. Running disaster scenarios on a loop. Burning through cognitive resources he needed for actual work. Poisoning his sleep. Straining his marriage. Preparing him for a catastrophe that existed only in his imagination.

By 11:00 AM Monday, he'd opened last week's client report and found three places where he'd rounded numbers differently than usual. *That's it. They found the mistakes. This meeting is about my sloppiness.*

By evening, he'd snapped at his wife over dinner, then withdrawn entirely, scrolling his phone while replaying every interaction with his manager from the past month. At 11:15 PM, he was lying in bed rehearsing explanations while his wife slept beside him, feeling completely alone, trapped in a catastrophe no one else could see.

By Tuesday morning, he was on high alert. Every interaction felt like evidence. His manager walked by without saying anything. *He's getting ready to fire me.*

By 1:45 PM, Marcus's hands were trembling. Heart pounding. Sweating despite the air conditioning. His body was in full threat mode, preparing him to fight or flee from a meeting that hadn't even happened yet.

At 2:03 PM, he walked into his manager's office, every muscle tense, braced for devastation.

His manager smiled. Gestured to a chair.

"Thanks for making time. I wanted to check in about the Morrison project. Leadership's impressed with your work. We'd like you to take the lead role. It'll be high visibility, great for your trajectory. Interested?"

Marcus stared. Blinked. His brain struggled to process words that didn't match twenty-eight hours of mental rehearsal.

"I… yes. Absolutely. Thank you."

He had spent over twenty-eight hours in emergency mode over a promotion.

THE SPIRAL YOU KNOW TOO WELL

Maybe your version looks different.

Maybe it's the text you sent three hours ago that got left on read. You've already written seventeen different explanations in your head, and fifteen of them end with "they hate me."

Maybe it's your teenager who came home from school and went straight to their room without saying hello. You're lying in bed at midnight convinced your relationship is falling apart, rehearsing the confrontation you'll have tomorrow, even though they probably just had a hard day and needed space.

Maybe it's Sunday at 7:43 PM and your chest is already tight about Monday morning. Not because anything specific is wrong, but because your brain has decided to preview every possible way the week could go sideways.

Maybe it's your partner who seemed "off" during dinner. Their face looked weird when they said "I'm fine." You're now spending the evening analyzing their tone, their body language, what they might have meant by that three-second pause, convinced they're about to leave you.

You know this trap. The way your mind can take one ambiguous moment and spin it into an entire catastrophic future. The way you can lie awake for hours solving problems that don't exist yet. The way you can ruin a perfectly good evening worrying about something that has a 2 percent chance of happening.

This isn't weakness. This isn't you being "too sensitive" or "overthinking things."

This is your brain doing exactly what evolution designed it to do.

The problem is, it's doing it in the wrong century.

The Spiral Cycle

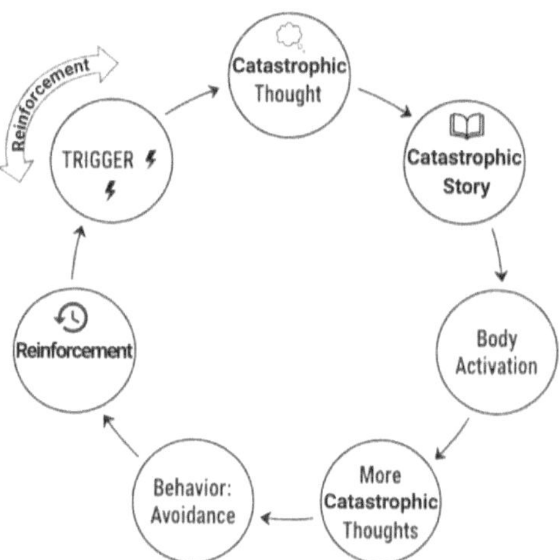

Figure 1: The Spiral Cycle - How catastrophic thinking creates a self-reinforcing loop

Not all anxiety is spiral-driven. Anxiety is the feeling; spiraling is the process of catastrophizing that amplifies that feeling. The Pivot interrupts the spiral, which helps regulate the anxiety.

WHY YOUR BRAIN DOES THIS (AND WHY IT'S NOT YOUR FAULT)

Here's the brutal evolutionary truth: your brain's primary job is not to make you happy. Its job is to keep you alive.

Every system in your brain evolved to answer one question: How do I survive long enough to reproduce?

Happiness? Optional. Creativity? Luxury. Peace of mind? Irrelevant. Survival? Non-negotiable.

This is why your brain prioritizes negative information over positive. Missing one threat could mean death. Missing one opportunity for joy just means slightly less joy. Better to be anxious and alive than happy and dead.

Your brain treats uncertainty as danger. In ancestral environments, the unknown was genuinely dangerous. New water sources might be poisoned.

Unfamiliar people might be hostile. Your brain learned: when in doubt, assume threat.

It favors familiar misery over unknown possibility.

You know you can survive this familiar pain. That unknown option might kill you. Your brain chooses the devil it knows.

This wiring served your ancestors brilliantly. The humans who survived long enough to become your ancestors were the ones whose brains were sufficiently paranoid, suspicious, and resistant to change.

You inherited their wiring.

And now you're trying to use that ancient survival operating system to navigate job interviews, creative projects, vulnerable conversations, and vague calendar invites.

It's a mismatch.

Your brain is still scanning for saber-toothed tigers. What it finds instead: passive-aggressive emails, ambiguous social cues, delayed text responses, unexpected meeting requests.

And because your brain can't tell the difference between physical danger and social uncertainty, it treats them the same way: **THREAT. ACTIVATE ALL SYSTEMS. PREPARE FOR WORST CASE.**

YOUR BRAIN'S PREDICTION MACHINE (AND WHY IT SABOTAGES YOU)

Right now, as you read this, your brain is running thousands of predictions per second: What word comes next? What does that sound mean? Is that movement a threat? What should I do in the next three seconds?

Neuroscientist Dr. Lisa Feldman Barrett describes the brain as a prediction machine, constantly forecasting what will happen next based on past experience.

When reality doesn't match your brain's prediction (when you expected your boss to smile and she frowned instead), the mismatch creates what neuroscientists call prediction error. Your brain reads that error as a threat.

This is where spirals start.

A coworker seems distracted during a conversation. Your brain scrambles to explain it: *Did I say something wrong? Are they upset with me? Did I miss something important?*

Never mind that they might be worried about a sick parent, distracted by an approaching deadline, or simply tired. Your brain defaults to the explanation that involves you being the problem, because if you're the problem, maybe you can fix it (illusion of control). If it's random, there's nothing you can do (terrifying).

Your brain would rather give you anxiety with control than peace with uncertainty.

Here's where this connects to manifestation and the Reticular Activating System (RAS): your brain's prediction machine and your RAS are running the same show. When manifestation teachers tell you to "focus on what you want," they're describing a real neurological process. Your RAS filters reality to show you what matches your expectations. If you're constantly predicting disaster, your brain will find evidence of disaster everywhere, not because you're "manifesting negativity," but because your prediction machine is scanning for threats, and your RAS is filtering for confirmatory data.

The problem isn't that manifestation doesn't work. The problem is that your nervous system is running threat predictions, and no amount of positive affirmations can override a brain in survival mode.

THE NEGATIVITY BIAS: WHY BAD STICKS AND GOOD SLIDES OFF

Imagine walking into a crowded room with 25 people. Over the course of the evening, you have conversations with all of them.

Twenty-four people tell you how amazing you are. They compliment your work, your ideas, your character. They're genuine. They mean it. Twenty-four people think you're exceptional.

But one person tells you they don't like you.

Maybe they criticize your work. Maybe they dismiss your ideas. Maybe they're cold, cutting, or just unimpressed.

One person out of twenty-five.

Here's my question: On your way home that night, which conversation are you thinking about?

When I do this exercise with live audiences, the response is always the same. The overwhelming majority say: they're thinking about the ONE negative conversation.

Not the 24 people who thought they were amazing. The ONE person who didn't like them. That's the conversation playing on repeat in their head.

Why?

Because negativity always comes to the front of the line in your mind.

Your brain doesn't weigh feedback equally. It doesn't average out the responses and conclude, "Well, 24 positive and 1 negative means I'm doing pretty well."

No. Your brain gives that one negative interaction VIP access. Front-row seat. Loudspeaker privileges. That one critical voice drowns out the other 24 like it's the only one that matters.

This isn't a character flaw. This isn't you being "too sensitive" or "unable to take criticism" or "needing thicker skin."

This is neurology.

Your brain is wired to prioritize threat over pleasure, danger over delight, criticism over praise. That ONE negative voice represents potential social rejection, which in our evolutionary past meant danger. So your brain fixates on it, replays it, analyzes it, catastrophizes about it, because at some point in human history, being rejected by the group could get you killed.

The problem? You're not living in a prehistoric tribe where social rejection equals death. You're living in the modern world where one person's opinion doesn't actually threaten your survival.

But your brain doesn't know that.

So it treats that one negative interaction like a five-alarm fire while the 24 positive interactions barely register as background noise.

This is why spirals feel so much more powerful than reality. One mistake at work can erase a year of excellent performance reviews in your mind. One critical comment from your partner can overshadow weeks of affection and support. One awkward social interaction can convince you that everyone thinks you're weird, even though dozens of other interactions went perfectly fine.

The negativity bias doesn't just make bad things feel worse than good things. It makes them louder, more persistent, more memorable. Negative experiences stick. Positive ones slide right off.

And here's what makes it even more insidious: you don't even realize it's happening. You genuinely believe you're seeing reality clearly. You think you're being "realistic" or "preparing for the worst" or "just being honest with yourself." But you're not. You're experiencing the world through a lens that magnifies threats and minimizes safety, amplifies criticism and mutes praise, highlights problems and obscures solutions.

Your brain is just doing what brains do.

But once you know this is happening, you can do something about it. You can't eliminate the negativity bias (it's hardwired into your neural architecture), but you can learn to recognize when it's running the show. You can learn to catch yourself mid-spiral and ask: "Am I seeing reality, or is negativity just at the front of the line again?"

That's what the Perspective Pivot teaches you to do. Not to ignore negative information or pretend everything is fine when it's not. But to reality-check whether the negative voice in your head is telling you the truth, or whether it's just doing what evolution designed it to do: scream louder than everything else.

Because most of the time? It's screaming.

And most of the time? You're listening to the wrong voice in the crowded room.

HOW SPIRALS MULTIPLY

Spirals start small. A seed of uncertainty: *I wonder why my boss wants to meet.*

Then multiply: *She probably found an error → that report must have been wrong → I didn't understand the assignment → I'm not qualified for this role → I've been faking competence → I'm getting fired → I'll never find another job → we'll lose the house → my kids' lives will be ruined because I'm a failure.*

Your body reacts to each leap as if it's already happening: racing heart, knotted shoulders, shallow breath, churning stomach, sleepless nights.

This isn't your body overreacting. It's responding exactly as designed. Your brain doesn't distinguish between imagined threats and real ones. When you catastrophize about getting fired, your alarm system activates the same stress response it would if you were actually being fired in that moment.

The cortisol flooding your system, the adrenaline spiking your heart rate, the tension locking your muscles—your body is experiencing the threat as real.

And here's what makes it worse: once your body is activated, your thinking brain starts to go offline. Blood flow shifts from your prefrontal cortex (rational thinking) to your amygdala (threat response). Your working memory shrinks. Your ability to see options narrows.

Your capacity for nuanced thinking disappears.

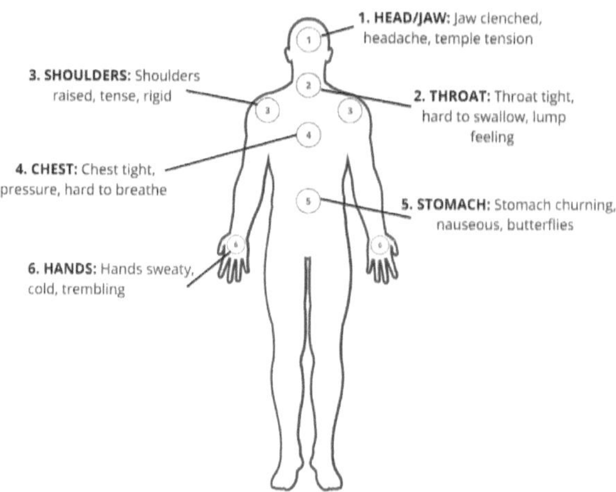

Figure 2: Where Spirals Show Up in Your Body - Common physical signs you're spiraling

For some brains, this happens faster and more intensely. If you've noticed that when you're stressed, you literally can't think (like your brain just stops) that's not you being weak. That's your nervous system prioritizing survival over cognition. Some brains hold onto executive function longer under stress. Others lose it immediately. Neither is better or worse. They're just different survival strategies.

THE FIVE PATTERNS YOUR BRAIN USES TO CATASTROPHIZE

Psychologist Dr. Aaron Beck identified predictable thinking patterns that fuel spirals. These aren't character flaws. They're evolutionary shortcuts your brain uses to process information quickly.

Understanding them is the first step to interrupting them.

Pattern 1: Mind Reading: "I know what they're thinking."
Your survival depended on quickly reading social cues to know who was friend or foe. Your brain would rather assume someone's frown means danger (and be wrong) than assume it's harmless (and get attacked). *Example: Marcus assumed the CFO checking his phone during presentations meant boredom with Marcus's work. Reality? A text from his daughter needing a ride.*

Pattern 2: Fortune Telling: "I know exactly how this ends."
Prediction helped your ancestors survive. Your brain is constantly running predictive simulations, but it always defaults to worst-case scenarios because preparing for disaster was safer than being optimistic. *Example: You prophesy disasters with cinematic detail, scripting entire catastrophic futures based on single uncertain moments.*

Pattern 3: Catastrophizing: "This small problem proves everything is ruined."
Your brain evolved to treat small threats as potentially existential. A minor injury in the wild could lead to infection and death, so your brain amplifies small problems, scanning for whether this could escalate.
Example: One critique becomes career doom. One mistake means total failure. A flat tire means the entire day is destroyed.

Pattern 4: All-or-Nothing Thinking: "If it's not perfect, it's worthless."
Binary thinking is fast. Safe/unsafe. Friend/enemy. Edible/poisonous.

When your ancestors had milliseconds to decide whether to run from a threat, nuance was a liability. Your brain still wants simple either/or answers. *Example: One B "ruins" your transcript. One stumble "proves" you're not leadership material.*

Pattern 5: Personalization: "Everything that goes wrong is my fault."

If you assumed everything was your fault, you could control it by changing your behavior. Your brain would rather believe you caused a problem (which means you can fix it) than accept that some things are outside your control (which means you're helpless). *Example: Your teenager's bad mood? Must mean you're a terrible parent.*

I've lived every one of these patterns, sometimes all before lunch. In reality, it was my nervous system begging for rest after years of over-functioning.

There were years when I'd walk out of meetings and spend the rest of the day dissecting every raised eyebrow or pause in conversation, convinced someone was disappointed in me. Before competing on The Blox, I spent nights scripting out my public downfall in full cinematic detail. When I hit burnout in 2019, I remember thinking, "Well, that's it. My career's over." One breakdown felt like a total collapse of identity.

And even now, when my teenager rolls their eyes, part of me still thinks, *What did I do wrong?* My brain wants control. It assumes if I caused it, I can fix it.

I share these because I don't teach this work from the mountaintop. I teach it from the middle, from the messy, human space of learning to recognize when my own brain is lying to me and choosing, one three-second window at a time, to pivot anyway.

WHAT MARCUS ACTUALLY LOST

Let's calculate what Marcus's three-day spiral cost him:

Productivity: Approximately 12 hours of work time lost to distraction and rehearsing disasters

Relationship: Snapped at his wife, withdrew from connection, disrupted her sleep with his insomnia

Physical: Tension headache, digestive issues, compromised immunity from stress hormones

Opportunity: Couldn't focus on actual work that would have impressed his manager further

Mental Energy: Depleted reserves he needed for genuinely difficult challenges

Confidence: Reinforced the belief that ambiguity equals danger, making future spirals more likely

That's the real tax of spirals: not just the suffering during them, but the life you don't live because you're consumed by threats that exist only in your imagination.

Think about the opportunities you didn't take because your brain convinced you they'd go badly. The conversations you didn't have because you were too busy rehearsing disaster. The risks you didn't pursue because uncertainty felt too dangerous. The joy you didn't feel because you were too activated to be present.

Your spiral voice isn't just stealing your peace. It's stealing your life.

WHY THIS IS GETTING WORSE RIGHT NOW

The specifics of what's happening in the world may change, but the overwhelm stays the same. Every generation has its version of uncertainty, but ours lives on a constant loop. Between economic shifts, social division, technological acceleration, and the endless noise of online comparison, our nervous systems rarely get to rest.

The human brain wasn't built for this level of input. It evolved to track a small circle of people and immediate surroundings, not thousands of voices, opinions, and crises competing for attention 24/7. Every notification, breaking headline, or "urgent" email pings the same circuitry that once kept your ancestors alive on the savanna.

We're living through unprecedented levels of ambient uncertainty. Your brain's ancient wiring is encountering more triggers in a single day than your ancestors encountered in a month.

Every notification is a potential threat. Every pause in conversation might mean disapproval. Every change at work could signal instability. Every global headline feeds the prediction machine looking for danger.

Your brain wasn't designed for this volume of ambiguity.

HOW MODERN LIFE HIJACKS YOUR BRAIN

And here's what almost no one is talking about: social media has turned your negativity bias into a full-time job. You're not just scanning your immediate environment for threats. You're scanning the entire world, 24/7, through a device that algorithmically serves you the most emotionally activating content because that's what keeps you scrolling.

Your RAS is supposed to filter reality to help you focus on what matters. Instead, it's being hijacked by infinite scroll, showing you every possible thing that could go wrong, everywhere, all at once.

No wonder you can't sleep. Your brain thinks it's monitoring threats for the entire human species.

THE COMPOUND COST

Think about the last month of your life.

How many hours did you spend lying awake catastrophizing? Replaying conversations, analyzing tone? Avoiding situations because your brain convinced you it would go badly? Managing anxiety about things that never happened? Preparing for disasters that didn't come?

Now multiply that by twelve months. By five years. By your lifetime.

That's not just lost time. That's a lost life.

Opportunities not taken because you talked yourself out of them. Relationships not deepened because you were too busy mind-reading. Creativity not expressed because perfectionism convinced you it wasn't good enough. Rest not taken because anxiety told you stillness was dangerous.

The spiral trap doesn't just steal your hours. It steals your potential.

And here's what makes this especially cruel: the more capable you are, the more sophisticated your spirals become. High-performing brains don't spiral less. They spiral in high definition. You can catastrophize in seventeen languages, simulate forty-three failure scenarios, and generate backup disasters in case the first ones don't pan out.

If you've ever thought, "I wish I could just turn my brain off," I get it. But here's the truth: the same brain that spirals brilliantly is also the brain that creates, solves problems, and sees patterns others miss. You don't need a different brain. You need to redirect the one you have.

THE INTERRUPTION POINT: FINDING THE SPACE

Holocaust survivor and psychiatrist Viktor Frankl discovered something profound in the most horrific conditions imaginable:

"Between stimulus and response there is a space. In that space is our power to choose our response. In our response lies our growth and our freedom." Viktor Frankl called it 'the space between stimulus and response.' I call it the three-second window. It's the same moment—the brief pause where choice lives.

Most of us let that space collapse instantly. Trigger hits, automatic reaction follows. We don't notice the moment where choice could exist.

But here's what I've learned: that space is always
there.

The calendar invite appears. For a fraction of a second, it's just information. Then your brain generates a story to explain your body's alarm response. Then the story crystallizes into certainty. Then confirmation bias activates, searching for evidence that supports the narrative.

The space exists between the trigger and the story. It shows up before your brain decides what the moment means.

It's brief, sometimes just milliseconds. But it's real.

And it's trainable.

You can't eliminate your alarm system. That would be dangerous and impossible. But you can learn to claim those crucial few seconds when your brain is generating a story but hasn't yet committed to one.

That's where the Perspective Pivot lives.

THE WAY OUT

Your anxious wiring once protected your ancestors. Your world requires different strengths: flexibility, perspective-taking, and wise action under uncertainty.

The solution isn't fighting biology. That's a war you'll lose.

The solution is working with your wiring in ways that serve the life you're actually living.

Marcus's spiral was predictable. His brain followed an ancient algorithm: uncertainty → assume threat → prepare for worst case → find evidence to support the story → repeat until resolved or exhausted.

But what if, in the space between seeing that calendar invite and spiraling into catastrophe, he'd had a tool?

What if he could have:

Acknowledged what was happening ("I'm catastrophizing about a meeting")

Adjusted his interpretation ("What else could 'check-in' mean?")

Aligned with wise action ("I'll respond professionally and wait for actual information")

Three steps. Three seconds. One pattern interrupt that could have saved him twenty-eight hours of suffering.

That's what the next chapter teaches you.

Not how to eliminate spirals —that's impossible. Instead, how to navigate them without being consumed. How to interrupt catastrophic thinking before it hijacks your day. How to claim the space between trigger and response so you can choose wisdom over panic.

Your brain will keep doing its threat-detection job.

But you're about to learn how to work with it instead of being controlled by it.

In the next chapter, you'll learn the exact three-step framework that claims that space between trigger and spiral. You'll practice it right in the chapter, so you walk away with a tool you can use immediately. The Perspective Pivot isn't theory. It's a practice that changes everything.

The spiral trap has been running your life long enough.

Let's build your way out.

* * *

KEY TAKEAWAY

Spirals aren't proof you're failing. They're evidence of ancient survival wiring misfiring in a modern context.

Your brain treats uncertainty as danger, prioritizes negative information, and generates catastrophic predictions to keep you safe.

When you understand the neuroscience behind catastrophic thinking, you stop taking it personally and start treating it as predictable biology you can learn to redirect.

* * *

TRY THIS

Think about your last major spiral—the one that stole hours or days from you.

Write down:

- **The trigger:** What happened that started the spiral?
- **The story:** What catastrophic narrative did your brain generate?
- **The cost:** What did this spiral actually steal from you? (time, sleep, relationships, opportunities, peace)
- **The outcome:** What actually happened? How accurate was your catastrophic prediction?

Most of the time, you'll discover: **the thing you spiraled about either didn't happen, or it was far less catastrophic than your brain predicted.**

That gap—between what you feared and what actually occurred—is where your freedom lives.

In the next chapter, you'll learn to claim it.

II

THE SOLUTION

2

The Three-Second Solution

"If you don't like the road you're walking, start paving another one."
— Dolly Parton

You know what a spiral feels like.

You know the sensation of your mind hijacking you, running catastrophic scenarios on a loop while your body floods with adrenaline over something that hasn't even happened yet. You've tried meditation apps that work when you're calm but disappear when you actually need them. You've tried positive affirmations that feel good until your next spiral proves they can't override biology.

You've tried thought records that work great after the fact but don't help when you're actively drowning.

Here's what you haven't tried: interrupting the spiral in the three-second window between trigger and catastrophe.

That's what this chapter teaches you.

Not a twenty-minute practice you'll never have time for. Not a complex therapeutic process that requires optimal conditions. A three-step framework you can execute in three seconds, anywhere, without anyone knowing you're doing it.

The Perspective Pivot isn't about eliminating anxiety. It's about transforming your relationship with it.

And it starts with understanding why three seconds is all you need.

Three seconds is the goal once the Pivot becomes automatic. When you're learning, it might take 30 seconds or a minute—that's perfect. Speed comes with practice.

THE WINDOW YOU'VE BEEN MISSING

Remember from Chapter 1: your brain defaults to catastrophe because evolution wired you for survival, not calm. When your alarm system detects a potential threat (a vague email, a frown, a change in plans), it activates faster than conscious thought. Your amygdala fires before your thinking brain even knows what's happening.

But there's a lag. A brief window, usually just seconds, between that bodily activation and when your brain locks onto a catastrophic explanation.

In those few seconds, your brain is scrambling to generate a story that explains why your body just activated. But that story hasn't yet crystallized into unshakeable certainty.

This is your window.

Most spirals happen because we miss it entirely. The catastrophic narrative forms so fast we never notice the moment where we could have chosen differently.

Your boss sends a vague email, your stomach drops, and by the time you consciously register what happened, you're already three sentences deep into "I'm getting fired."

The Perspective Pivot teaches you to **catch that window and claim it.**

Three steps. Three seconds. One choice that redirects your entire nervous system.

In other words, your alarm system fires first, and the Pivot is how you bring your thinking brain back online before the spiral takes over.

WHAT HAPPENS IN YOUR BRAIN DURING A THREAT

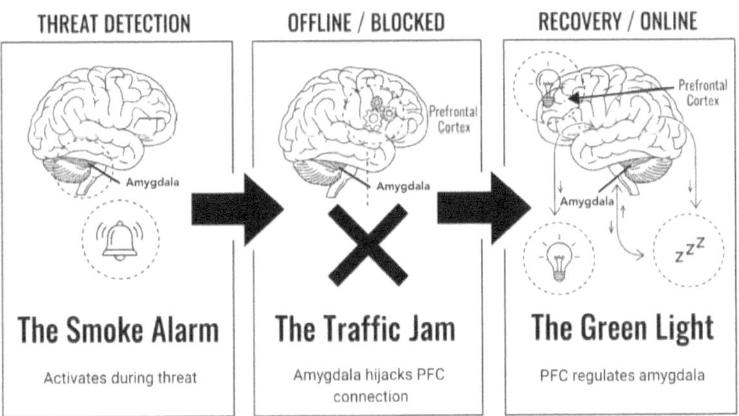

Figure 3: What Happens in Your Brain - The amygdala activates during threat, and the Pivot reconnects your prefrontal cortex

THE FRAMEWORK: ACKNOWLEDGE, ADJUST, ALIGN

Think of the Perspective Pivot like a traffic light for your brain.

- **ACKNOWLEDGE = Red light.** Stop. Notice what's happening.
- **ADJUST = Yellow light.** Pause. Consider alternatives.
- **ALIGN = Green light.** Move forward with intention.

Simple. But simple doesn't mean easy, and it definitely doesn't mean simplistic.

Let me show you what's actually happening in each step.

Step 1: Acknowledge

What you do: Name what's happening. Out loud or in your head.

Why it works: When you put feelings into words (even just thinking "I'm anxious right now") you activate your prefrontal cortex (your thinking brain) which automatically quiets your amygdala (your alarm system). UCLA researchers found that simply labeling what you are feeling can cut amygdala activation roughly in half.

What to acknowledge: The emotion you're feeling: "I'm anxious." "I'm scared." "I'm angry."

What your body is doing: "My chest is tight." "My heart is racing." "My stomach is clenched."

What story your mind is telling: "I'm having the thought that I'm going to fail." "My spiral voice is saying they hate me."

What you're NOT doing: Judging yourself for feeling this way. Trying to make it stop Pretending you're fine. You're simply noticing and naming what's true right now.

Example:

Marcus (remember him from Chapter 1?) gets a vague email from his boss: "Check-in tomorrow at 2pm."

Old pattern: immediate spiral. "I'm in trouble.

What did I do wrong? I'm getting fired."

New pattern with Acknowledge: "My stomach just dropped. My body activated. My spiral voice is saying I'm in trouble. I'm having the thought that this is bad news."

Notice the difference? He's not saying the thought is true. He's saying he's having the thought. That tiny shift creates space between him and the spiral, and that space is where choice lives.

Common mistake: Moving your fingers without naming anything.

Fix: Don't move to the next step until you've put at least one emotion, sensation, or thought into words.

Step 2: Adjust

What you do: Ask yourself, "What else could this mean?"

Why it works: Your brain's first explanation for uncertain situations is usually the scariest one because negativity comes to the front of the line. But your brain is guessing. It doesn't actually know why your boss sent that vague email.

The Adjust step does two things:

- **First:** Generate other possible explanations. Not to convince yourself everything is fine, but to remind your brain that its first scary guess isn't the only possibility.
- **Second:** Check the story against actual evidence.

This isn't toxic positivity. It's reality-checking.

Example:

Marcus moves to Adjust: "What else could this mean? My boss might want my input. They might want to check on workload. They might have an opportunity. This could be routine."

Then he checks the story against evidence: "My last three performance reviews were strong. My boss praised me last week. This company doesn't surprise-fire people."

He's not convincing himself it's good news. He's breaking the certainty that it's bad news. That matters, because spirals feed on certainty, not facts.

Step 3: Align

What you do: Choose one small action that matches who you want to be.

Why it works: You can't think your way into new patterns. You have to act your way into them.

Neuroscientists call this "self-directed neuroplasticity," which is a fancy way of saying your brain rewires itself based on what you repeatedly do.

Ask yourself:

"Given this broader view, what's one action that reflects who I want to be?"

Example:

Marcus moves to Align: "What would the calm, competent version of me do right now?"

Action: "Finish my current task with focus. Close my laptop at 6. If I think of a question, I'll send it tomorrow."

The action doesn't solve everything. It reflects his values instead of his fear.

The next day, his boss wants his opinion on a new vendor. Nothing catastrophic.

Total spiral time: 90 seconds instead of three days

THE TRIPLE-A HAND HACK: MAKING IT PHYSICAL

Here's the problem with mental techniques: when your alarm system fully activates, your thinking brain goes partially offline.

That's why I developed the Triple-A Hand Hack. Three simple gestures that anchor each step of the Pivot in your body so the technique remains accessible even under extreme pressure

The Triple-A Hand Hack

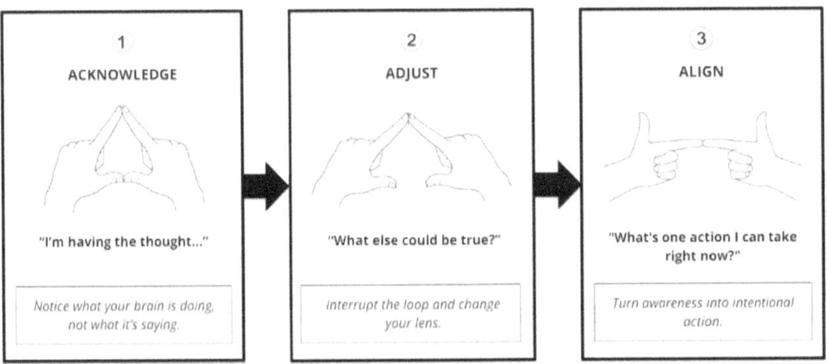

Figure 4: The Triple-A Hand Hack - Physical gesture to anchor each step of the Pivot

WHY PHYSICAL ANCHORS WORK

When threat floods your system, your thinking brain (prefrontal cortex) goes offline. But your motor patterns (physical movements you've practiced) remain accessible through different neural pathways. Your basal ganglia (which stores motor habits) doesn't shut down under stress the way your prefrontal cortex does.

This is why athletes practice the same movements thousands of times. Under game pressure, when conscious thought is too slow, their bodies execute automatically. The Triple-A Hand Hack works the same way.

Research by Dr. Susan Goldin-Meadow at the University of Chicago shows that physical movements while thinking actually enhance cognitive processing and emotional integration. The gestures aren't decorative.

They're the mechanism that makes the Pivot accessible when you need it most.

THE THREE GESTURES

Gesture 1: Acknowledge

The move: Bring the tips of your thumbs and index fingers together to form a triangle, an "A" shape.

The meaning: You're naming what's real. The triangle symbolizes awareness and stability.

The cue phrase: "Catch the thought. Change the direction."

Why it works: The "A" for Acknowledge creates a closed circuit, a physical anchor for pause and recognition. The pressure activates mechanoreceptors (touch sensors) in your fingertips, sending signals to your somatosensory cortex. This tactile feedback grounds you in physical sensation when your mind is spiraling into catastrophic futures.

While making this gesture, name what's true: "I'm feeling anxious." "My mind is jumping to worst-case scenarios." "My chest is tight and my heart is racing."

Common mistake: Touching too briefly (quick tap, immediately moving on). *Fix:* Hold the gesture for at least 1-2 seconds. Take a full breath while maintaining contact.

ACKNOWLEDGE

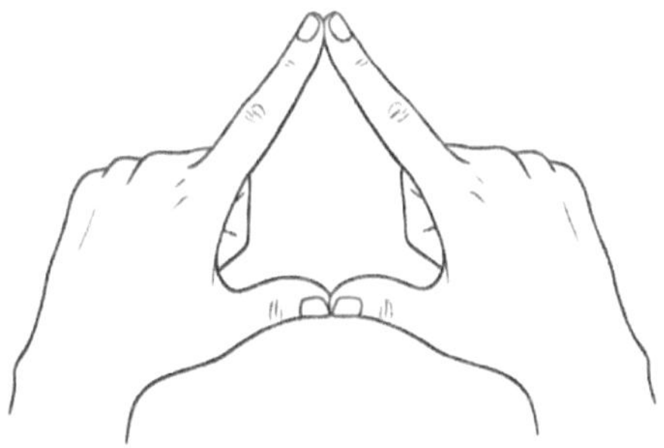

Figure 4a: Acknowledge hand position

Gesture 2: Adjust

The move: Keep your index fingers touching but separate your thumbs, breaking the triangle apart.

The meaning: You're creating space to pivot, symbolically breaking the old pattern and inviting a new perspective.

The cue phrase: "Ask: What else might be true?"

Why it works: Breaking apart represents releasing grip, opening to possibility. When you're spiraling, your perception narrows to threat. The physical act of breaking the connection mirrors the mental act of breaking free from catastrophic certainty.

While making this gesture, ask: "What else could be true here?" Then generate at least two or three alternative interpretations for whatever triggered you.

Common mistake: Rushing through alternatives (generating one alternative and moving on). *Fix:* Force yourself to come up with at least three possibilities before proceeding.

ADJUST

Keep index fingers touching, but separate thumbs, breaking the triangle.

Figure 4b: Adjust hand position

Gesture 3: Align

The move: Rotate your hands so your index fingers point towards each other, touching tip to tip, with your thumbs now pointing upwards.

The meaning: You're directing your focus forward, toward intentional action instead of rumination.

The cue phrase: "Awareness starts the shift.

Alignment makes it real."

Why it works: This parallel alignment creates a bridge, a unification of all parts of yourself. After acknowledging what's true and adjusting your interpretation, you need to integrate that wisdom and point yourself toward action.

While making this gesture, ask: "Given this broader view, what's one action that aligns with who I want to be?" "What would the calm, wise version of me do right now?"

Common mistake: Choosing multiple actions (creates overwhelm). *Fix:* Choose ONE action only. Use the "can I do this in the next hour?" test. If not, it's too abstract.

ALIGN

Figure 4c: Align hand position

THE COMPLETE SEQUENCE

Executed fully, the sequence takes three seconds: **Second 1:** Touch →
Acknowledge **Second 2:** Break → Adjust

    Second 3: Align → Act

    Extended Version (20–30 seconds): Use breaths.

    Lightning Version (1–2 seconds): Subtle in public.

    Invisible Version: Imagine the gestures; motor imagery activates similar
brain regions, so you still get the benefit.

TRY IT RIGHT NOW

Before you continue reading, practice the complete sequence with me. Right
now, wherever you are:

Touch your thumbs to your index fingertips, forming an "A"

Feel the contact. The pressure. The pause this creates.

Say to yourself (out loud or silently): "I'm learning something new. I'm feeling [whatever you're actually feeling right now: curious, skeptical, hopeful, overwhelmed]. This matters to me."

Take one full breath while maintaining the gesture.

Break your thumbs apart

Feel the expansion. The opening. The release of the closed position.

Say to yourself: "This practice will take time. I won't be perfect. Progress will be messy. And that's exactly as it should be. I can learn this."

Bring your index fingers together, parallel, pointing toward each other

Feel the alignment. The direction. The bridge between both sides.

Say to yourself: "The very next time I notice my spiral voice spinning a catastrophic story, I'll use this technique. Not perfectly. Just sincerely."

There. You just did it.

Your first Pivot. The first three seconds of building a skill that will serve you for the rest of your life.

Did it feel awkward? Good. New skills always do.

Did you feel silly? That's your brain resisting change because change feels unpredictable and unpredictable feels unsafe.

Did it seem too simple to actually work? That's exactly why it works. Complexity fails under pressure. Simplicity persists.

THE PIVOT IN ACTION: THREE REAL EXAMPLES

Elena's Boardroom Blank

Elena, 42, healthcare administrator, was presenting to her hospital's executive team when her mind went completely blank. Just gone. Silence stretched. Fifteen executives stared at her, waiting.

She'd been practicing the Pivot.

Acknowledge (subtle movement at the podium): "My mind went blank. This is embarrassing. My heart is pounding."

Adjust: "This is human. It happens to everyone. Authenticity might actually land better than perfection."

Align: She smiled, made eye contact, and said: "Well, looks like my brain decided to take a coffee break. Give me just a moment to find my place."

The room laughed. With her, not at her. Someone said, "We've all been there."

Elena found her thread and continued. Several executives commented afterward on her poise under pressure.

Sarah's Sunday Night Protocol

Sarah, 34, had anticipatory anxiety about Monday's commute that hijacked every Sunday evening. After learning the Pivot, she created a proactive protocol.

7:30 PM on Sunday: *Acknowledge:* "Tomorrow is Monday. My chest is beginning to tighten. This is anticipatory anxiety about something that hasn't happened yet."

Adjust: "I've handled Monday commutes before. If I hit traffic, I can text my team. Some of this anxiety is just transition from weekend to workweek."

Align: "I'm setting my alarm 10 minutes earlier and making a podcast playlist. Then I'm going to enjoy what's left of my Sunday."

The dread that used to steal her entire Sunday evening now lasted about five minutes.

Jamie and the Unanswered Text

Jamie sent a text to a friend three hours ago. No response. Old pattern: spiral. New pattern: *Acknowledge:* "I'm feeling anxious. My spiral voice is saying they're mad at me." *Adjust:* "They might be in a meeting. This friend has been reliable for two years." *Align:* "I'm going to finish this work task with focus. If I don't hear back by tonight and it's time-sensitive, I'll send a gentle follow-up."

Friend responded four hours later: "Sorry! Phone died during a client meeting."

Total time spiral lasted: 60 seconds instead of four hours.

WHY THIS WORKS WHEN OTHER THINGS DON'T

It intervenes during the spiral while your brain is still forming the story.

It uses physical anchors that remain accessible when thinking fails.

It works with your wiring instead of against it.

It is simple enough to execute anywhere, in three seconds.

It builds evidence through action, not just reflection.

FOR MY NEURODIVERGENT READERS

If you have ADHD, autism, or another neurodivergent wiring, this often works even better for you. Here's why:

Executive function challenges make abstract techniques hard. Physical anchors bypass that.

Sensory sensitivity enhances the tactile grounding.

Pattern recognition strengths help automate the sequence faster.

Time blindness makes the "three seconds" flexible— timing doesn't matter, sequence does.

RSD intensifies spirals — naming that intensity creates space.

We'll dive deeper into adaptations in Chapter 5. If you need those tools now, skip ahead and return here. By the time neurodivergent readers reach Chapter 5, this framework will already feel familiar.

Note for Neurodivergent Readers: If executive function, working memory, or sensory overwhelm makes any step difficult, skip to Chapter 5 right now for specific adaptations, then return here.

YOUR FIRST PRACTICE

Think of a situation from the past week that triggered catastrophic thinking. A text with no response. A facial expression you interpreted negatively. A decision made with incomplete information. A mistake that felt bigger than it was. Anticipatory anxiety about something coming up.

Now run it through the Pivot.

Step 1: Acknowledge

What were you feeling? What was your body doing? What story was your spiral voice telling?

Step 2: Adjust

What else could have been true? What evidence did you ignore?

Step 3: Align

What is one action the calm, wise version of you would have taken?

You just did a retrospective Pivot.

It felt clunky? Perfect. Skills feel clunky before they feel natural.

What happens next: you practice. Not perfectly. Not obsessively. Just consistently enough that your brain learns a new pattern.

Every time your spiral voice starts spinning catastrophe, you have a choice: repeat the loop or claim your three-second window.

Ready To Practice?

- **For structured practice:** Appendix C (30-Day Challenge)
- **For quick reference:** Appendix A (Quick Reference Guide)
- **For real-world examples:** Appendix D (Case Studies)

Or continue reading for advanced techniques and adaptations.

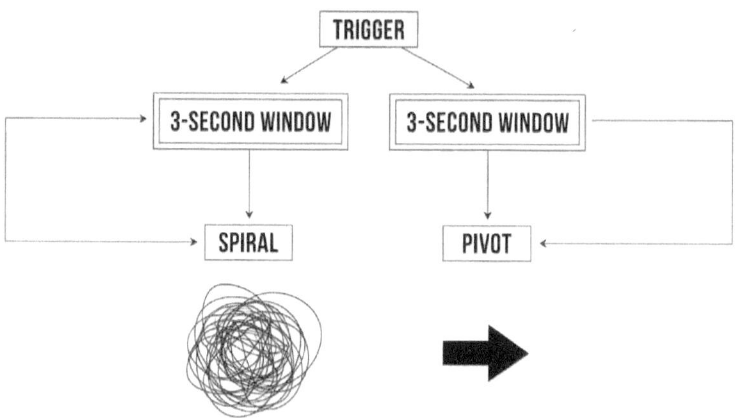

Figure 5: The Three-Second Window - The moment where you can choose to spiral or pivot

In Chapter 3, you'll get the complete toolkit that expands the Pivot into every corner of your life.

Right now, you have everything you need to start.

Three steps. Three seconds. One choice that changes everything.

Welcome to the revolution.

* * *

KEY TAKEAWAY

The three-second window between trigger and spiral is your freedom. In that brief space, your brain is generating a story to explain your body's alarm response, but that story hasn't yet crystallized into catastrophic certainty.

The Perspective Pivot teaches you to claim that window with three steps: ACKNOWLEDGE what is true, ADJUST your interpretation by generating alternatives, and ALIGN by taking one small action that reflects who you want to be.

The Triple-A Hand Hack gives you physical anchors (forming a triangle, breaking it apart, and aligning your fingers forward) that remain accessible even when your thinking brain goes offline.

This isn't about eliminating anxiety. It's about transforming your relationship with it.

* * *

TRY THIS

Think of one situation from this past week that triggered catastrophic thinking. Run it through the complete Pivot right now:

- **ACKNOWLEDGE (touch thumbs to index fingers forming triangle):** What were you actually feeling? What was your body doing? What story was your spiral voice telling? Write it down or say it out loud: "I was feeling . My body was . My spiral voice was saying ."

- **ADJUST (break thumbs apart):** What else could have been true about that situation? Generate at least three alternative explanations. Force yourself, even if they feel less compelling than your catastrophic interpretation.
- **ALIGN (index fingers parallel, pointing forward):** Based on that broader view, what's one action you could have taken (or could still take) that would reflect your values instead of your fear?

You just ran your first retrospective Pivot. It might have felt awkward or artificial. That's normal when building a new skill. The more you practice, the more natural it becomes. Your next step: commit to practicing this sequence once per day for the next week, using past spirals as practice material. You're building the neural pathway so it's there when you need it most.

3

Adjust & Align

"We don't see things as they are; we see things as we are."
— Anaïs Nin

You know the basic framework now. Acknowledge, Adjust, Align. Three steps that interrupt spiraling in real time.

But here's what nobody tells you about learning a new skill: the basic version gets you started, but mastery requires depth.

Think about learning to cook. You can follow a recipe and make something edible. But understanding why ingredients work together, how heat transforms food, when to trust your instincts over the instructions, that's when you become a cook instead of just someone following directions.

The Perspective Pivot works the same way.

Chapter 2 gave you the recipe. This chapter gives you the chef's knowledge, the additional techniques and troubleshooting strategies that make the Pivot work in every situation life throws at you.

DEEPENING THE ACKNOWLEDGE STEP

Most people rush through Acknowledge. They want to skip straight to feeling better, so they do a quick "yeah, I'm anxious" and jump to Adjust.

But Acknowledge is where the real power lives.

When you truly acknowledge what's happening (not just surface feelings but the layers underneath) you give your nervous system permission to shift. Rushing through it is like trying to build a house without laying the foundation.

The Timeline Reality Check

Your spiral voice loves to collapse time. It makes right now feel like forever.

You made one mistake, and suddenly your brain is fast-forwarding to: "I'll never recover from this. My reputation is ruined. I'll be dealing with consequences for years."

But here's what's actually true: you're experiencing one moment. One situation. One challenge.

When you're acknowledging, add this question: "How long has this actually been happening?"

You got a critical email five minutes ago. Not five months. Five minutes.

You had an awkward interaction this morning. Not all morning. One three-minute conversation this morning.

Your friend hasn't texted back yet. It's been three hours. Not three days. Three hours.

This isn't minimizing your feelings. It's giving your nervous system accurate information about the scope of the situation.

Dr. Rick Hanson, neuroscientist and author, talks about how our brains are "Velcro for negative experiences and Teflon for positive ones." Negative experiences stick and expand in our minds. Positive experiences slide right off.

The Timeline Reality Check interrupts that expansion. It reminds your brain: this is one moment, not your entire life.

EXPANDING THE ADJUST STEP

Adjust is where most people get stuck. They understand they're supposed to generate alternative explanations, but their catastrophic interpretation feels so real that everything else seems fake.

Let me give you additional tools to make Adjust more powerful.

The Percentage Question

When your spiral voice makes an absolute claim ("This will definitely fail," "They definitely hate me," "I'll never recover") ask yourself: "What percentage certain am I?"

Not 100% or 0%. Actually pause and consider: If you had to bet money, what would you honestly estimate?

Your spiral voice says: "My manager is definitely going to fire me."

You pause and ask: "What percentage certain am I that this is true?"

Maybe it's 70%. Maybe it's 40%. Maybe, when you're really honest, it's 15%.

Now ask: "What does that percentage tell me?"

If you're 70% certain, that means there's a 30% chance you're wrong. That's not nothing, that's nearly one in three.

If you're 40% certain, that means you're more likely to be wrong than right.

If you're 15% certain, your spiral voice is catastrophizing about something that's statistically unlikely.

The point isn't to eliminate uncertainty. It's to right-size it.

Your spiral voice treats 15% probability like 100% certainty. It makes you feel and act as if the worst case is inevitable when it's actually improbable.

When you quantify your certainty, you activate your prefrontal cortex, the thinking part of your brain that deals in probabilities and nuance. This interrupts the amygdala's black-and-white threat assessment.

Then you can adjust: "I'm 15% certain I'll get fired, which means I'm 85%

certain I won't. My anxiety is treating the 15% like it's guaranteed. But probability doesn't work that way. I'm responding to a low-likelihood scenario as if it's already happening."

Marcus might use this when spiraling about his boss's vague email:

Acknowledge: "I'm catastrophizing that I'm in trouble."

Adjust: "If I'm honest, I'm maybe 30% certain that email means something bad. That's less than a coin flip. I'm having a full panic response to a scenario I'm actually 70% confident ISN'T happening."

Align: "I'm going to respond to the email normally and see what actually unfolds, rather than acting on the 30% worst-case possibility."

The Evidence Lawyer

Pretend you're a lawyer building a case. But instead of prosecuting yourself, you're defending yourself against the charges your spiral voice is making.

Your spiral voice says: "I'm terrible at my job."

You, as the Evidence Lawyer, respond: "That's a sweeping generalization unsupported by facts. Let's examine the actual evidence."

Then you list specific, concrete evidence that contradicts the catastrophic claim:

"Last month, my manager praised my work on the Henderson account. Three weeks ago, a client specifically requested me for their project. Yesterday, I solved a problem that had been stalling the team for days. Last quarter, I exceeded my performance targets."

Notice: these aren't affirmations. These aren't "I'm amazing" statements. These are facts. Verifiable, specific facts.

Your spiral voice will try to dismiss this evidence. "Yeah, but that was just luck" or "They were just being nice" or "That doesn't count because..."

That's when you respond: "You're moving the goalposts. The original claim was 'I'm terrible at my job.' The evidence clearly shows competent, valued work. If you want to revise your claim to something more specific, like 'I made a mistake on this one thing,' we can discuss that. But the original charge is factually inaccurate."

This technique comes from Cognitive Behavioral Therapy (CBT), specifically the work of Dr. Aaron Beck and Dr. David Burns. They discovered that depression and anxiety aren't caused by situations themselves, but by the distorted interpretations we make about situations.

When Trauma Amplifies Your Spirals

Here's something most self-help books won't tell you: your alternatives feel fake sometimes because they're bumping up against unresolved trauma or deeply held beliefs about yourself.

If you grew up in a household where love was conditional on achievement, your brain learned: "Mistakes mean rejection."

So when you make a mistake at work now, your brain doesn't just think "I made a mistake." It thinks "I'm about to be abandoned."

That's not catastrophic thinking. That's trauma pattern activation.

If you experienced bullying, criticism, or betrayal in your past, your brain built protective predictions: "People who seem friendly now will turn on me eventually." "If I let my guard down, I'll get hurt." "Trust is dangerous."

So when a friend takes three hours to text back, your brain doesn't think "They're busy." It thinks "Here it comes. They're pulling away. I knew this would happen."

The Adjust step can't fully work until you acknowledge these deeper patterns.

Try adding this question to your Adjust practice: "Is this triggering an old wound?"

If your spiral feels disproportionate to the situation (you're having a massive emotional response to something objectively small) that's often a clue that you're not just responding to what's happening now. You're responding to what happened before.

Marcus might realize: "This vague email is triggering my childhood experience of my dad's silent treatment before punishment. Uncertainty meant something bad was coming. My body learned that pattern thirty years ago, and it's still running."

That awareness doesn't make the fear disappear. But it creates space to say: "My body is responding to a thirty-year-old pattern. My boss is not my father. This workplace is not that household. The old pattern might not apply here."

Your spiral voice isn't random. It's constructed from messages you received, experiences you survived, and conclusions you drew to keep yourself safe. Your spiral voice isn't your enemy. It's trying to protect you using strategies that worked once but don't fit anymore.

When you're in Adjust, try asking: "What is my spiral voice trying to protect me from?"

The answer reveals what you need to address with compassion, not just logic.

If your spiral voice is catastrophizing rejection, it might be protecting you from the pain of being blindsided. It's saying "If I expect the worst, at least I won't be surprised."

You can acknowledge that protection: "My spiral voice is trying to keep me from being hurt. That makes sense given my history."

Then adjust: "But living in constant bracing causes its own kind of pain. The protection has become the problem. I can handle uncertainty without catastrophizing it. I've done it before."

This is where therapy can be incredibly valuable. If you notice the same spirals triggering again and again despite using the Pivot, there might be deeper work to do around the wounds underneath. The Perspective Pivot is a powerful tool for real-time regulation. But it's not a replacement for addressing unresolved trauma with a qualified therapist.

STRENGTHENING THE ALIGN STEP

Align is where insight becomes action. It's where you move from understanding to embodiment.

But here's where people get stuck: they choose actions that are too big, too vague, or too focused on managing discomfort instead of moving toward values.

The Micro-Action Test

When you're choosing your Align action, ask: "Could I do this in the next hour?"

If the answer is no, it's too big.

"I'm going to completely restructure my relationship with anxiety" is not an Align action. It's a therapy goal.

"I'm going to send one email I've been avoiding" is an Align action.

"I'm going to stop being such an overthinker" is not an Align action. It's a wish.

"I'm going to finish this paragraph without checking my phone" is an Align action.

Align actions should be small, specific, and immediately doable.

Why? Because your nervous system needs evidence that you can navigate uncertainty. One small action provides that evidence. A huge overwhelming goal just creates more anxiety.

Every time you take a small aligned action, you're proving to yourself: I can do hard things. I can act wisely even when I'm scared. I can move forward despite uncertainty.

Those small proofs accumulate. That's how transformation happens, not through one massive change, but through hundreds of tiny aligned choices.

The Values Compass

Sometimes you don't know what aligned action to take because you're not clear on your values.

Your values are not the same as your goals. Goals are destinations. Values are directions.

"Get promoted" is a goal. "Contribute meaningfully to work I care about" is a value.

"Find a partner" is a goal. "Show up authentically in relationships" is a value.

"Stop being anxious" is a goal. "Act courageously despite fear" is a value.

When you're choosing an Align action, ask: "What do I value in this area of my life?"

If the trigger is work-related, maybe you value competence, contribution, or integrity.

If the trigger is relationship-related, maybe you value honesty, connection, or kindness.

Then choose an action that moves you toward that value, even if it's tiny.

Marcus values competence and clear communication. So when he gets that vague email, his Align action might be: "I'm going to respond professionally if I have questions, rather than spiraling silently."

That's an action that reflects his values, regardless of what the email actually means.

The Opposite Action

Sometimes the wisest aligned action is the exact opposite of what your anxiety is screaming at you to do.

Your anxiety says: avoid. Wisdom says: engage.

Your anxiety says: withdraw. Wisdom says: reach
out.

Your anxiety says: overexplain and defend.

Wisdom says: stay calm and curious.

This comes from Dialectical Behavior Therapy (DBT), developed by Dr. Marsha Linehan. She discovered that when emotions don't fit the facts of a situation, acting opposite to the emotional urge can actually change the emotion.

If you're anxious about a social event and your urge is to cancel, the opposite action is to go (even if just for 15 minutes).

If you're angry and your urge is to lash out, the opposite action is to speak calmly or take space before responding.

If you're ashamed and your urge is to hide, the opposite action is to share vulnerably with someone safe.

Elena, standing at that podium with her mind blank, felt the urge to panic and shut down. Her opposite action was to acknowledge the moment with humor and grace. That opposite action changed everything.

TROUBLESHOOTING COMMON OBSTACLES

Let me address the problems people run into when practicing the Pivot.

"I forget to use it until after I've already spiraled"

This is the most common issue, especially in the beginning.

Solution: Start with retrospective Pivots. At the end of each day, think of one moment when you spiraled. Run it through the framework after the fact.

This builds the neural pathway even when you're not doing it in real time. Your brain starts recognizing the pattern: trigger, spiral, opportunity to pivot.

Eventually, you'll catch yourself mid-spiral. Then early-spiral. Then right at the trigger.

"My catastrophic thought feels so real that alternatives feel fake"

This means you're trying to convince yourself the catastrophic thought is wrong instead of acknowledging it might be partly true while also seeing it's not the whole truth.

Try this reframe: "This thought might be one possibility. It's not the only possibility. And I can't know which possibility is accurate until I have more information."

You're not saying the catastrophe definitely won't happen. You're saying you don't have enough information yet to know what will happen.

That's not fake. That's actually more accurate than certainty in either direction.

I call this the **Both/And Reframe** — the practice of holding "this might be true" and "other things might also be true" at the same time, without forcing a verdict before you have enough information. It sounds small, but it is genuinely powerful.

"I can Acknowledge and Adjust fine, but I don't know what action to Align with"

Start smaller. If you can't figure out the perfect aligned action, just choose: one breath. One question. One moment of not checking your phone.

The action doesn't have to solve everything. It just has to reflect intention instead of reaction.

"This works for small stuff but not when I'm really triggered"

That's because you're trying to run before you can walk.

You don't practice the Pivot for the first time during a crisis. You practice it on small frustrations (traffic, a delayed text, a minor annoyance) so the neural pathway is established before high-stakes situations hit.

Think of it like learning to swim. You don't start in the ocean during a storm. You start in the shallow end.

Then the deep end. Then calm open water. Then you're ready for waves.

FOR MY NEURODIVERGENT READERS

ADHD-specific considerations for the Toolkit:

Working memory challenges might make it hard to remember all these additional techniques. That's fine. Pick one. Practice that one until it's automatic. Then add another.

You don't need to master every tool in this chapter. You need to deeply internalize the ones that work for your brain.

The Evidence Lawyer technique can trigger perfectionism spirals if you're not careful. Remember: you're not building a case that you're perfect. You're building a case that the catastrophic claim is inaccurate.

Autism-specific considerations for the Toolkit:

Alexithymia (difficulty identifying emotions) might make emotion-labeling challenging. That's okay. Start with what you can identify, even if it's just "something feels wrong in my chest."

Concrete thinking might make the "Who Do I Want to Become?" question feel too abstract. Try this reframe: "What would [person I admire] do in this situation?" Make it specific and external.

Pattern recognition strengths mean these techniques might click suddenly once you've practiced enough times. Your brain will recognize the pattern and automate it. Trust that process.

You now have the complete toolkit.

Chapter 2 gave you the framework. This chapter gave you the depth, the additional techniques and troubleshooting strategies.

But here's what nobody tells you about skills: knowing them doesn't make you good at them. Practice makes you good at them.

In Chapter 4, I'm going to show you exactly how to practice. How to make the Pivot automatic so it's there when you need it most, without having to consciously remember it.

Because the goal isn't to become someone who's good at using this technique when you remember.

The goal is to become someone who pivots instinctively when spirals start, the same way you instinctively catch yourself when you trip.

But transformation requires more than understanding—it requires automation. **That's what we build next.**

* * *

KEY TAKEAWAY

The basic Perspective Pivot framework gets you started, but mastery requires depth.

Acknowledge works best when you add Timeline Reality Checks (how long has this actually been happening?).

Adjust becomes more powerful with the Percentage Question (what percentage certain am I?), the Evidence Lawyer technique (building a factual case against sweeping generalizations), and recognizing when past trauma or personal biases are amplifying current spirals.

Align requires micro-actions you can complete in the next hour, values-based choices instead of fear-based avoidance, and sometimes choosing the opposite action from what anxiety demands.

These additional tools don't replace the basic framework, they deepen it so the Pivot works in every situation life throws at you.

* * *

TRY THIS

Pick one of the advanced techniques from this chapter and practice it right now:

- **The 25 People in the Room:** Think of your most recent spiral thought. Imagine 25 people who know you well hearing your spiral voice say that thought out loud. Picture their faces. How many would agree? How many would look confused? How many would actively disagree? Write down that number. The gap between what your spiral voice says and what people who actually know you would say is where truth lives.
- **The Evidence Lawyer:** Take one sweeping catastrophic claim your spiral voice made recently ("I'm terrible at my job" or "I always mess everything up"). Now build a defense case with specific, verifiable evidence that contradicts it. List at least five concrete facts that disprove the sweeping claim. Notice how your certainty about the catastrophic thought shifts when you demand actual evidence.
- **The Micro-Action Test:** Think about a current situation causing anxiety. What aligned action could you take in the next hour? Not a huge overwhelming solution—one small, specific, immediately doable action that reflects your values. Write it down. Then do it. Notice how taking one small aligned action shifts your nervous system even when the situation isn't resolved.

Practice one of these techniques daily for the next week. Depth comes through repetition, not through trying to use all techniques simultaneously.

You now have the complete toolkit. In Chapter 4, we build the one thing that makes all of it work under pressure: automaticity.

68

III

MAKING IT LAST

4

Making It Automatic

When I first started practicing the Perspective Pivot, I wanted it to be instant. I thought if I just understood it deeply enough (if I taught it, wrote about it, lived it) then my brain would magically default to it in real time.

It didn't.

For months, I still spiraled. I still woke up in fight-or-flight, checked my email before my nervous system had even caught up to my body, and told myself I "should" know better by now. I'd stand in my kitchen at 6 AM, heart racing about something that hadn't even happened yet, and think: *I literally teach this. Why can't I just do it?*

Knowing the science didn't save me from being human.

It took time (messy, inconsistent, deeply uncomfortable time) for the Pivot to become muscle memory. Some days, I'd catch myself mid-spiral and use the hand hack: thumbs and index fingers together, forming that triangle while standing in my kitchen or sitting in my car, feeling slightly ridiculous but doing it anyway. It worked, but it required every ounce of conscious effort.

Other days, I'd forget everything I teach and fall face-first into old habits. I'd spiral for hours before remembering I had a tool. I'd catastrophize about catastrophizing. I'd feel like a fraud for teaching something I couldn't consistently practice.

But slowly (so slowly I didn't even notice it happening) repetition rewired me. The same tools I built to help others started working on me without me forcing them.

I realized one day, standing in line at a coffee shop anxious about an upcoming meeting, that I'd automatically paused and thought: *I'm nervous. My chest is tight. This is anticipation, not prophecy. What else could be true? This could go fine. I've done this before. I can handle whatever happens.*

Then I ordered my coffee.

The whole thing took maybe three seconds. I hadn't consciously decided to use the Pivot. I hadn't formed the triangle with my hands or recited the steps. It had just happened. My brain had done it on its own.

It was small and ordinary, and it stopped me in my tracks.

I stood there with my latte thinking: *That just worked. Without me thinking about it. The Pivot is actually in there now.*

The truth is, I didn't master the Perspective Pivot because I invented it. I mastered it because I needed it. My recovery wasn't a clean, linear rise. It was a series of

micro-pivots (moments of falling apart and coming back to center, over and over) until coming back to center became the default instead of the exception.

That's the real work. That's what practice looks like: not perfection, but remembering, again and again, that you can always begin within three seconds.

Even when you forget for hours.

Even when you spiral despite knowing better. Even when you're the one teaching it.

This chapter is about closing the gap between understanding the Pivot and embodying it. Between knowing what to do and actually doing it when your nervous system is activated and your spiral voice is screaming.

It's about making the Pivot automatic. Not perfect, but accessible. Not always smooth, but always available.

Because the goal isn't to never spiral. The goal is to know how to find your way back.

Let me show you how.

WHY WILLPOWER DOESN'T WORK

Here's why most people fail to turn the Pivot into a habit: they rely on remembering to use it in the moment.

But spiraling hijacks your prefrontal cortex (the part of your brain responsible for memory, planning, and conscious decision-making). When your alarm system activates, your brain can't access learned techniques the way it can when you're calm.

That's why automaticity matters.

When a skill becomes automatic, it transfers from your prefrontal cortex (conscious, effortful) to your basal ganglia (unconscious, automatic). The same part of your brain that lets you drive to work on autopilot while thinking about your day.

Once the Pivot is stored in your basal ganglia, you don't have to remember to use it. Your body initiates it before your conscious mind even registers the trigger.

That's the goal. And there's a specific path to get there.

THE FOUR STAGES OF SKILL DEVELOPMENT

Psychologists who study expertise have identified four stages everyone goes through when learning a new skill. Understanding these stages helps because you'll know what's normal and when you're actually making progress.

Stage 1: Unconscious Incompetence

You don't know what you don't know. This was you before you picked up this book. You were spiraling regularly but didn't realize there was a three-second window you were missing.

You've already moved past this stage.

Stage 2: Conscious Incompetence

You know what to do, but you can't do it yet. This is where most people are after reading Chapters 2 and 3. You understand the framework, but when you're actually spiraling, you forget it exists until twenty minutes later.

This stage feels frustrating. You know better, but you're not doing better yet. This is completely normal. Stay here. This is where the work happens.

Stage 3: Conscious Competence

You can do it, but it requires effort and attention. This is when you start catching yourself mid-spiral. You still have to consciously remember to do it. It's not automatic yet. But you're doing it more often, and it's starting to work.

This stage is exciting because you're seeing results.

But it's also tiring because it requires constant vigilance.

Stage 4: Unconscious Competence

You do it automatically without thinking about it. This is mastery. The Pivot becomes your default response to uncertainty. A trigger happens, and before you're even consciously aware of it, your hands are already forming the triangle gesture and your brain is already running through Acknowledge.

You still spiral sometimes. But the spirals are shorter, less intense, and you recover faster.

Most people reach this stage after 60 to 90 days of consistent practice. Not

60 days of perfect practice. 60 days of sincere, imperfect, messy practice.

Here's what that actually looks like:

- **Week 1-2:** You'll catch spirals hours later and think, 'I could have used the Pivot there'
- **Month 1:** You'll catch spirals mid-spin and successfully interrupt them sometimes
- **Month 2-3:** You'll start catching spirals at the trigger point before they fully form
- **Month 4-6:** The Pivot becomes automatic—you do it without consciously deciding to
- **Beyond 6 months:** You develop 'spiral immunity'—triggers that used to hijack you barely register"

THE PROGRESSIVE PRACTICE PROTOCOL

Here's how you build automaticity: you practice in progressively more challenging conditions. You don't learn to pivot for the first time during a crisis. You build the skill in calm waters, then gradually introduce waves.

The complete 30-Day Perspective Pivot Challenge with daily prompts, tracking sheets, and progressive practice scenarios is in Appendix C. But here's the framework:

Week 1: Foundation Practice in Calm States

You're not using the Pivot on real spirals yet. You're building the neural pathway in controlled conditions.

Daily practice: 5 minutes when you're relatively calm. Morning works for most people.

Run through the Triple-A Hand Hack three times:

- ***Round 1:*** Physical practice only. Form the triangle, hold for three breaths.

Separate thumbs, hold for three breaths. Bring index fingers parallel, hold for three breaths. You're teaching your hands the sequence.

- **Round 2:** Add internal dialogue. Triangle: "I'm practicing a skill that will serve me." Separation: "This will take time. That's exactly as it should be." Alignment: "I'm choosing to invest in my own regulation."
- **Round 3:** Use a past spiral from yesterday. Run it through the full framework using the gestures.

Why this works: You're practicing the sequence until your hands and brain know the pattern, like learning scales before playing a song.

Week 2: Application to Low-Stakes Frustrations

Now you start using the Pivot on real situations, but small ones. Traffic. Slow Wi-Fi. Minor annoyances that activate you slightly but aren't emotionally overwhelming.

Goal: Catch yourself within 30 seconds of activation.

These small activations are perfect practice because the stakes are low, they happen frequently, and they're predictable. You can even plan: "When I hit traffic today, I'm going to practice the Pivot."

Common experience: You'll forget to use it most of the time. You'll remember three hours later. That's fine.

Each time you remember (even late) you're strengthening the pattern.

Week 3: Integration into Genuinely Challenging Situations

Now you're ready for medium-stakes spirals. An email that triggers worry. A conversation that leaves you replaying it all evening. Anticipatory anxiety about something coming up.

Goal: Catch yourself within 5 minutes of spiral starting.

You won't catch it at the trigger yet. You'll catch it mid-spiral. This is huge progress. You're developing metacognition (the ability to observe your own thinking).

Practice tip: Set random alarms on your phone three times a day. When the alarm goes off, pause and ask: "Am I spiraling right now?" If yes, pivot immediately. If no, run through a quick preventive pivot.

Week 4: Mastery Through High-Stakes Implementation

By week four, you're using the Pivot on the spirals that matter most. Work performance. Relationship conflicts. Health scares. Financial stress.

Goal: Notice the trigger before the spiral fully forms. This is where automaticity starts to emerge. You feel your body activate, and before your mind has constructed the full catastrophic story, your hands are already forming the triangle. You're catching the window.

What mastery actually looks like: You'll still spiral sometimes. But now you notice within seconds instead of minutes. You'll still have catastrophic thoughts. But now they feel like weather passing through instead of absolute truth. You'll still get activated. But now you recover in minutes instead of hours or days.

This isn't elimination. It's skilled navigation.

BUILDING THE DAILY PRACTICE HABIT

The practice protocol works if you actually do it. Here's how to make practice inevitable:

Anchor it to an existing habit. After your morning coffee. Right after you brush your teeth. During your commute. The existing habit becomes the trigger.

Make it ridiculously easy. Commit to three minutes, or even one minute. The goal is consistency, not optimization.

Track it visually. Get a calendar. Every day you practice, mark an X. Your only goal: don't break the chain.

Research by Dr. Phillippa Lally found that habits take an average of 66 days to become automatic. Some habits automated in 18 days. Others took 254 days. The only factor that predicted automaticity: consistency, not perfection. Missing one day didn't derail the process.

Missing two days in a row started to weaken the neural pathway.

TROUBLESHOOTING THE PRACTICE PROCESS

"I practiced for a week and then completely forgot about it"

You didn't build the practice into your environment.

Solution: Put physical reminders everywhere. A note on your bathroom mirror. An alarm on your phone. Make the practice visible.

"I practice during calm moments but still can't access it when I'm activated"

This is the conscious competence stage. You're right on track. The gap closes through repetition. Keep practicing in calm moments while also attempting to use it during low-stakes activation.

"I feel silly doing the hand gestures"

Do you feel sillier doing three seconds of hand gestures, or spending three hours spiraling about something that never happens? Also, you can do the gestures subtly or invisibly. Nobody needs to know you're regulating your nervous system.

"I used it successfully a few times, then had a massive spiral where I completely forgot"

This isn't regression. This is normal skill development. Learning follows a pattern: small wins, big setback, more small wins, smaller setback, more wins, tiny setback, consistency. The setbacks don't mean you've lost the skill.

"I'm practicing consistently but not seeing results"

Define results. If you're expecting to never spiral again, that's not realistic. If you're expecting to spiral less intensely and recover faster, that's measurable.

Try this: Before you start practicing, write down your typical spiral pattern. How long does it usually last? How intensely do you feel it (1-10 scale)? After two weeks, measure again. Comparing week 0 to week 2 reveals progress you might not notice day to day.

FOR MY NEURODIVERGENT READERS

ADHD-Specific Practice Considerations:

Habit formation takes longer with ADHD. Research shows it can take 50 to 100 percent longer for ADHD brains to automate new behaviors. This doesn't mean it won't work. It means you need more repetitions. Don't compare your timeline to neurotypical timelines. 90 days for them might be 120 to 150 days for you.

Working memory challenges mean you'll forget to practice more often. External reminders are even more critical. Set multiple alarms. Put visual cues everywhere. Make it impossible to miss.

Novelty-seeking tendencies mean you might get bored with the same practice routine. That's fine. Rotate your practice scenarios. Practice with different past spirals. Practice in different locations. Keep it varied.

Time blindness means you might think you've been practicing for weeks when it's been four days. Track it externally. The calendar X method is crucial for ADHD brains.

Autism-Specific Practice Considerations:

Routine and predictability are strengths here. Once you establish the practice routine, your brain will likely stick to it more consistently than neurotypical brains. But rigidity can backfire if life disrupts your routine. Build flexibility into your practice from the start. Have a primary practice time and two backup times.

Pattern recognition means once you've practiced enough times, your brain will lock onto the sequence and automate it quickly. Trust that process. You might hit automaticity faster than expected once critical mass is reached.

Alexithymia might make the Acknowledge step harder because you struggle to name emotions. Start with body sensations instead. "My chest is tight" is just as valid as "I feel anxious."

Concrete thinking means abstract concepts like "values" feel slippery. Create concrete definitions. Write down specific behaviors that reflect your values. Make it observable and external.

THE PIVOT JOURNAL: ADVANCED TRACKING

If you want to accelerate your progress, add one more practice: the Pivot Journal.

Every day, answer these three questions:

1. ***Today I spiraled about:*** One sentence. Be specific. Not "work stuff" but "the email from my boss about the Henderson project."
2. ***I caught myself:*** Never / After hours of spiraling / Within an hour / Within minutes / At the trigger

You're tracking your awareness speed. This is how you measure progress objectively.

1. ***What I learned:*** One insight from today's spiral or pivot. Maybe you noticed a pattern. Maybe you discovered a new trigger.

This takes two minutes. After two weeks, read back through your entries. You'll see patterns and progress you didn't notice day to day.

WHAT COMES AFTER AUTOMATICITY

Here's what people don't tell you about mastery: it's not a destination. It's a deepening.

Even after the Pivot becomes automatic, you'll keep discovering new layers. You'll notice subtler triggers. You'll catch spirals earlier. You'll develop your own variations and adaptations.

You'll have setbacks. Stressful life events will temporarily knock you back to conscious competence. That's normal. The skill doesn't disappear. You just need to re-engage it consciously until it re-automates.

The goal isn't to never spiral again. The goal is to become someone who recovers quickly, learns from each spiral, and gets slightly better at navigation over time.

In Chapter 5, we're going to address the specific adaptations you need if your brain works differently.

Because while the core Pivot framework is universal, neurodivergent brains need specific modifications to make it work optimally.

If you have ADHD, autism, or another form of neurodivergence, the next chapter is for you.

And even if you're neurotypical, read it anyway. Because understanding how the Pivot adapts for different neurologies will deepen your understanding of how your own brain works.

The practice starts now. Not tomorrow. Not when you feel ready. Now.

Pick one moment from today that activated you.

Run it through the Triple-A Hand Hack right now, as you're reading this.

That's your first practice rep. Do it again tomorrow.

And the day after.

Sixty days from now, you'll be a different person.

Not because anxiety disappeared, but because you learned to navigate it skillfully.

That's the revolution.

* * *

KEY TAKEAWAY

Knowing the Perspective Pivot and being able to use it when you're activated are two completely different skills.

Automaticity happens through progressive practice in increasingly challenging conditions, not through willpower or trying to remember in crisis moments.

The four stages of skill development (unconscious incompetence, conscious incompetence, conscious competence, and unconscious competence) take most people 60 to 90 days of consistent practice to reach.

- Week 1 focuses on calm practice building the neural pathway.
- Week 2 applies the Pivot to low-stakes frustrations.
- Week 3 integrates it into genuinely challenging situations.
- Week 4 involves high-stakes implementation where you start catching triggers before spirals fully form.

The goal isn't perfection. It's building the skill so deeply that pivoting becomes as automatic as catching yourself when you trip.

* * *

TRY THIS

Start your progressive practice protocol today:

Week 1 Foundation Practice (do this right now, then daily for 7 days):

Find 5 minutes when you're relatively calm. Run through the Triple-A Hand Hack three times:

- **Round 1 - Physical only:** Form the triangle, hold for three breaths. Separate thumbs, hold for three breaths. Bring index fingers parallel, hold for three breaths. You're teaching your hands the pattern.
- **Round 2 - Add dialogue:** Triangle: "I'm practicing a skill that will serve me." Separation: "This will take time. Progress won't be linear." Alignment: "I'm choosing to invest in my own regulation."
- **Round 3 - Use a past spiral:** Think of something from yesterday that triggered you. Run through the full Acknowledge-Adjust-Align framework using the gestures.

Track it: Get a calendar. Mark an X every day you practice. Your only goal: don't break the chain. Aim for no more than one missed day per week.

Anchor it: Attach this practice to something you already do daily (after morning coffee, before bed, during your commute). The existing habit becomes the trigger for the new habit.

After 7 days of calm practice, move to Week 2: applying the Pivot to low-stakes frustrations like traffic or slow wifi. You're building automaticity through repetition in progressively challenging conditions.

5

The Neurodivergent Pivot

"I am not broken. I am not incomplete. I am not less than. I am different, and that difference is not a deficit."
— Devon Price

If you have ADHD, autism, or another form of neurodivergence, I need you to hear something before we go any further.

This chapter isn't an afterthought. It's not a "special accommodations" section tacked onto a book designed for neurotypical brains. This entire book was built with your brain in mind from the ground up.

The Triple-A Hand Hack exists because abstract cognitive techniques don't work when executive function is offline. The physical anchors bypass the parts of your brain that struggle under stress.

The three-second framework exists because long, multi-step processes are impossible when you're overwhelmed. Three steps is the maximum your working memory can hold when you're activated.

The emphasis on body-based regulation exists because your nervous system has been running at capacity your entire life, and traditional "just think

84

differently" approaches have failed you repeatedly.

You're not an edge case in this work. You're the prototype.

Everything in this book works better for neurodivergent brains because it was designed around the challenges neurotypical people only experience occasionally but you experience constantly.

So this chapter isn't about how to modify the Pivot to work for you. It's about understanding why it already does, and how to optimize it even further for your specific neurology.

WHY SPIRALS HIT DIFFERENTLY FOR NEURODIVERGENT BRAINS

Let's start with why the spiral trap is deeper for you. It's not because you're "more anxious" or "overthink more" than neurotypical people. It's because your baseline nervous system activation is already higher before you even encounter a trigger.

The Baseline Difference

Dr. Russell Barkley's research on ADHD shows that ADHD brains operate with lower levels of norepinephrine and dopamine in the prefrontal cortex. This creates a baseline state of restlessness, distractibility, and emotional intensity.

Dr. Temple Grandin's work on autism reveals that autistic brains process sensory information differently, often without the typical filtering that neurotypical brains do automatically. This creates a baseline state of sensory overload even in "normal" environments.

So when a spiral trigger hits, you're not starting from zero. You're starting from 60.

A neurotypical person encounters a vague email from their boss. Their nervous system goes from 0 to 40. Uncomfortable, but manageable.

You encounter the same email. Your nervous system goes from 60 to 100. That's not just uncomfortable. That's overwhelming.

And here's what makes it worse: you've been masking this your entire life. You've learned to appear calm externally while your nervous system is screaming internally. The energy it takes to mask leaves less energy for actual regulation. By the time you notice you're spiraling, you're already deep in it.

ADHD AND THE SPIRAL AMPLIFICATION

If you have ADHD, spirals hit you with unique intensity because of how your brain processes emotion, time, and working memory.

Rejection Sensitive Dysphoria (RSD)

Dr. William Dodson's clinical work reveals that RSD isn't just "being sensitive to criticism." It's a neurological difference in how your brain processes perceived rejection. When someone with ADHD experiences criticism, their brain registers it as: "This is devastating. This is unbearable. I can't survive this." It's not emotional weakness. It's a difference in how intensely emotional pain registers neurologically.

The Perspective Pivot helps because Acknowledge gives you permission to name that intensity without judgment. Not "I shouldn't feel this devastated over a small criticism," but "My RSD is activated. This feels unbearable. That's my neurology, not evidence that the criticism is accurate." That tiny reframe creates space.

Time Blindness and Working Memory

ADHD brains struggle with time perception. What happened five minutes ago and what happened five years ago can feel equally present. When you're spiraling about a mistake you made this morning, your brain is also pulling up every similar mistake from the past decade.

They all feel like they're happening right now.

Your working memory (the mental space where you hold and manipulate information) is also smaller with ADHD. This is why the Pivot is three steps, not seven.

ADHD Adaptations:

The Timeline Reality Check: When you're spiraling, physically write down: "This happened [specific time]. It lasted [specific duration]. It is not still happening now." External time markers help because your internal time sense is unreliable.

The One-Step Emergency Pivot: When you're so overwhelmed that even three steps feels impossible, just do Acknowledge. Form the triangle. Name what's happening: "I'm completely overwhelmed. My brain is chaos. I can't think straight." That's enough. You don't have to Adjust or Align when you're in crisis mode.

Emotional Dysregulation and Recovery Time

ADHD brains take longer to return to baseline after emotional activation. A neurotypical person's cortisol returns to baseline in 20 to 30 minutes. Yours might stay elevated for hours. Your nervous system doesn't have the "off switch" working as efficiently.

Using the Pivot successfully doesn't mean you feel calm immediately. It means the spiral doesn't continue escalating, and you shorten the recovery window from hours to maybe 60 to 90 minutes. That's still success.

AUTISM AND THE SPIRAL COMPLEXITY

If you're autistic, spirals function differently because of how your brain processes social information, change, and sensory input.

Social Ambiguity as Constant Trigger

Neurotypical social communication relies heavily on unstated context, implied meaning, and nonverbal cues. For autistic brains, this creates constant uncertainty. Every social interaction is a potential spiral trigger because ambiguity activates your threat system.

Someone says "That's interesting" about your work. Does that mean they're genuinely interested? Politely dismissing you? Being sarcastic? You literally can't tell. Your brain scrambles to generate explanations. Without clear data, it defaults to threat.

Autism-Adapted Adjust:

Standard Adjust: "What else could this mean?"

Autistic-adapted Adjust: "I don't have enough data to know what this means. My brain is guessing. I can't solve this puzzle with the information I have."

You're acknowledging insufficient data. That stops your brain from committing to a catastrophic interpretation based on incomplete information.

Then your Align action becomes: "I can ask a clarifying question" or "I can let this ambiguity exist without needing to solve it immediately."

Change As Threat

Autistic nervous systems often perceive change as threat, even when the change is neutral or positive. Your boss announces a schedule change. Even if the new schedule is actually better, your nervous system activates because routine was disrupted.

This isn't about being "rigid." It's about how your brain processes unpredictability.

When change triggers a spiral, your Acknowledge step needs to include: "A change happened. My nervous system registers change as threat. This is my neurology responding to unpredictability, not evidence that the change is actually dangerous."

Sensory Overload and Spiral Threshold

Your sensory processing is different. Sensory dysregulation lowers your spiral threshold. If you've been in a loud, bright environment for hours, your nervous system is already maxed out. A tiny trigger that wouldn't normally cause spiraling now sends you over the edge.

Autistic-Adapted Practice: Sensory Baseline Tracking

Before you use the Pivot, do a quick sensory check: "On a scale of 1 to 10, how close am I to sensory overload right now?"

If you're at 8 or above, the Pivot might not work because your nervous system is too dysregulated. In that case, regulation comes before Pivot. Remove yourself from the sensory environment if possible. Reduce input. Engage your sensory regulation tools (headphones, weighted blanket, dim lights).

Once you're back down to a 5 or 6, then you can attempt the Pivot.

Alexithymia and Emotional Labeling

Many autistic people experience alexithymia, difficulty identifying and naming emotions. This makes the Acknowledge step challenging.

Autistic-Adapted Acknowledge:

Instead of: "I feel anxious."

Try: "My chest is tight. My stomach is churning.

My hands are cold. Something feels wrong but I can't name it."

That's valid Acknowledge. You're naming your experience accurately. You don't need an emotion label for the Pivot to work.

HEALING THE NERVOUS SYSTEM

Here's something critical that most anxiety books miss: you can't just "manage" a dysregulated nervous system. You have to actually heal it. And for neurodivergent brains, your nervous system has been running in survival mode for years, maybe decades.

The Cost of Chronic Activation

Living in a world not designed for your neurology means your nervous system has been in threat mode constantly. Every time you had to mask your natural behaviors.

Every time sensory input overwhelmed you but you had to keep functioning. Every time executive function failed but you were punished for it.

Your nervous system learned: the world is not safe. I must stay vigilant. I cannot relax.

That chronic activation changes your physiology.

Your baseline cortisol runs higher. Your amygdala becomes hyperactive. Your vagus nerve (the nerve that helps you shift from threat mode to rest mode) loses flexibility.

Dr. Stephen Porges's Polyvagal Theory explains this: your autonomic nervous system has three states.

Ventral vagal: Safe and social. Your nervous system is calm.

Sympathetic: Fight or flight. Your nervous system is activated.

Dorsal vagal: Shutdown. Your nervous system is overwhelmed. You freeze or dissociate.

Neurodivergent nervous systems might get stuck in sympathetic or collapse into dorsal vagal more easily because of chronic activation.

Building Nervous System Capacity

Healing doesn't mean your nervous system becomes neurotypical. It means it gains more flexibility and resilience within your neurology.

Key practices:

Co-regulation: Your nervous system learns safety through connection with other regulated nervous systems. Intentionally spend time with calm, accepting people when you're not in crisis. Their nervous system signals to yours: "It's safe here."

Bilateral stimulation: Alternating left-right movement (walking, tapping knees alternately, butterfly hug). This helps your brain process stress.

Vagal tone exercises: Humming or singing.

Vibration in your throat activates your vagus nerve, which shifts your nervous system from threat to safety.

Gentle movement: Yoga, tai chi, stretching. Not intense exercise. Slow, mindful movement that helps you feel your body.

Weighted pressure: Weighted blankets, tight hugs, compression clothing. Deep pressure activates your parasympathetic nervous system and signals safety.

Window of tolerance work: Dr. Dan Siegel's concept: the zone where you can function effectively.

Neurodivergent windows are often narrower. Nervous system healing widens your window so you have more room to navigate without sliding into dysregulation.

The key: these practices work best when done regularly in non-crisis moments.

ADHD-Specific Nervous System Healing

Movement as medicine: ADHD brains need movement for regulation. When spiraling, movement can help more than sitting still. Walk. Pace. Dance. Bounce. Let your body discharge activation. Then attempt the Pivot.

Stimulation regulation: Find the right stimulation level. Not too little (restless and dysregulated). Not too much (overwhelmed and dysregulated). Moderate caffeine, screen time with boundaries, physical activity that's energizing but not exhausting.

Autism-Specific Nervous System Healing

Sensory diet: Work with an occupational therapist to develop daily sensory routines that keep your nervous system regulated (weighted blanket in morning, crunchy snacks midday, hot shower in evening).

Predictability as regulation: Build routines around regulation. Same morning sequence. Same wind-down routine. Your nervous system regulates better with predictability.

Unmasking as healing: Find spaces where you can unmask. Let yourself stim. Avoid eye contact when it's uncomfortable. Say "I don't understand" when you don't. Your nervous system will learn: I can exist as I am. That's safety.

THE NEURODIVERGENT PIVOT IN ACTION

ADHD Example: *The Hyperfocus Crash Spiral*

Jamie has ADHD. They hyperfocused on a project for six hours, forgot to eat, and now they're crashing hard.

A text comes in from a friend: "Hey, can we reschedule coffee tomorrow?"

Old pattern: Immediate RSD activation. "They don't want to see me. I'm annoying. Our friendship is over."

Neurodivergent Pivot:

- *Acknowledge (Triangle gesture):* "My RSD just activated. This feels devastating. My nervous system is already depleted from hyperfocus. I'm hungry and dysregulated. The text feels like rejection but I'm in survival mode right now."
- *Adjust (Break thumbs apart):* "I don't have enough information. They said reschedule, not cancel. Have they rescheduled before? Yes. Did it mean friendship was ending? No."
- *Align (Fingers forward):* "I'm going to eat something first. Then I'll respond to the text. My nervous system needs regulation before I can assess this accurately."

Jamie eats. Nervous system stabilizes. The devastation fades to mild disappointment.

They text back: "No problem! How about Thursday instead?"

Friend responds: "Perfect! Just had a work thing come up."

Total spiral duration: 15 minutes instead of three

days.

Autism Example: The Change Announcement Spiral

Alex is autistic. Their manager announces: "Starting next month, we're switching to a new project management system."

Old pattern: Immediate overwhelm. "I just learned the old system. Now I have to learn a new one. I won't be able to do my job. I'm going to fail."

Neurodivergent Pivot:

- *Acknowledge (Triangle gesture):* "Change was announced. My nervous system is activated. I'm experiencing change-as-danger, which is my neurology. My body is tight. I want to shut down."
- *Adjust (Break thumbs apart):* "I don't have enough information to know if

this is actually dangerous. I've learned new systems before. It was hard but I managed."

- *Sensory check:* "Am I already at sensory capacity? Yes, the office is loud today."
- *Align (Fingers forward):* "I'm going to put on my headphones to reduce sensory input first. Then I'm going to ask my manager: when is training? Will there be written instructions? Can I have extra time to learn?"

Alex asks the questions. Manager says training is in three weeks, there will be step-by-step guides, and they can practice in a sandbox environment first.

Alex's nervous system calms. The change still isn't fun, but it's not catastrophic.

PDA (Pathological Demand Avoidance) Considerations

If you experience PDA (where everyday requests trigger intense demand avoidance) the Pivot needs additional modification. The language "you should" or "you need to" might trigger avoidance even when you're telling yourself.

Reframe the Pivot as choice, not demand:

- **Instead of:** "I need to acknowledge what I'm feeling."
- **Try:** "I could notice what's happening right now if I want."
- **Instead of:** "I should generate alternatives."
- **Try:** "I wonder what else might be true here?"
- **Instead of:** "I have to align with my values."
- **Try:** "What would feel good to do right now?"

The softer language reduces demand pressure while still allowing access to the same regulatory pathway.

WHEN THE PIVOT ISN'T ENOUGH

Let me be direct: the Perspective Pivot is powerful, but it's not a replacement for other support you might need.

If you're experiencing chronic depression that makes getting out of bed impossible, trauma responses that flood your system regularly, severe anxiety that disrupts daily functioning despite using every tool in this book, or suicidal thoughts, you need professional support beyond this book.

The Pivot can work alongside therapy and medication. It's not instead of those things. Therapy helps you process the deeper wounds. Medication can stabilize brain chemistry. The Pivot gives you a real-time navigation tool. All three working together create the strongest foundation.

For crisis-specific protocols, see Chapter 6. For professional support resources, see Appendix B

YOUR NEURODIVERGENT ADVANTAGE

Here's what I need you to understand before we close this chapter.

Your neurodivergence isn't a deficit you have to overcome to use the Pivot. It's often an advantage.

Your pattern recognition helps you identify spiral triggers faster once you know what to look for.

Your intensity means when you commit to practicing the Pivot, you practice deeply.

Your need for systems and structure means you're more likely to build consistent practice habits.

Your sensory awareness means you notice body activation earlier, giving you more time to intervene.

The world tells you your brain is wrong. This book tells you your brain is different, and that difference makes you better at some things, including this work.

Author Story: The Day My Diagnosis Made Everything Make Sense

I was thirty when I got diagnosed with ADHD. Thirty. Old enough to have built a career, earned a doctorate, and collected every label from "driven" to "disorganized," but young enough for the truth to completely rewrite the story I'd been telling myself.

At first, it felt like relief. Finally, there was a reason for the mental chaos, the missed details, the emotional intensity that always felt one notch higher than everyone else's. But that relief quickly gave way to grief. Because once I understood how my brain actually worked, I couldn't stop wondering how different things might have been if someone had seen it sooner.

I remember sitting alone in my car after that appointment, fingers clenched around the steering wheel, a mix of anger and sadness flooding through me. My brain went straight into overdrive: *How did you not know? How much time did you waste trying to fix something that was just wired differently?*

I didn't have the tools I have now. I hadn't built the Perspective Pivot yet. But even then, instinctively, I started doing what I now know was the first step: I acknowledged what was happening. I stopped fighting the storm in my head long enough to name it: grief, relief, and exhaustion all tangled together. And for the first time, I gave myself permission to feel it instead of forcing myself to "power through."

That moment didn't fix everything. But it cracked something open in me. It was the first time I saw that maybe the way my brain worked wasn't the enemy, maybe it was the clue. Years later, surrounded by other entrepreneurs at The Blox, I would start connecting those dots, realizing that reframing how we see ourselves could completely change how we think, lead, and live. That's where The Perspective Pivot was born.

But this (sitting in my car at thirty, realizing my brain was responding exactly as it should) this was the seed. It was the first time I began to understand that perspective isn't about pretending everything's fine. It's about learning to see yourself through a different lens when your mind insists on the old one.

In Chapter 6, we're going to address what happens when life delivers genuine crisis. Not just spirals, but actual hard things. Job loss. Relationship endings. Health scares. Grief. Because the Pivot isn't just for managing catastrophic thoughts about things that might happen. It's also for navigating actual hard things that do happen.

* * *

KEY TAKEAWAY

The Perspective Pivot wasn't designed for neurotypical brains with neurodivergent adaptations added as an afterthought. It was built with neurodivergent brains in mind from the ground up.

Physical anchors work when executive function is offline. Three-step simplicity fits working memory limitations. Body-based regulation addresses chronic nervous system activation.

For ADHD brains: acknowledge Rejection Sensitive Dysphoria intensity without judgment, use timeline reality checks to counter time blindness, and allow the One-Step Emergency Pivot (just Acknowledge) when overwhelmed.

For autistic brains: start with body sensations instead of emotion labels if you experience alexithymia, acknowledge change-as-threat as neurology not rigidity, do sensory baseline checks before attempting the Pivot, and reframe steps as choice not demand if you experience PDA.

Nervous system healing through co-regulation, somatic practices, and widening your window of tolerance makes the Pivot more accessible.

Your neurodivergence isn't a deficit to overcome.

It's often an advantage in this work.

* * *

TRY THIS

Identify your specific neurodivergent adaptations:

If you have ADHD:

Next time you feel devastated by something small, pause and ask: "Is this RSD activation?" Practice this Acknowledge: "My RSD is activated. This feels unbearable. That's my neurology, not evidence that the situation is actually catastrophic."

Write down three instances where you successfully handled criticism or perceived rejection before. Keep this list accessible for when RSD hits. Your brain's time blindness makes past evidence invisible—external lists make it visible.

Try the One-Step Emergency Pivot next time you're overwhelmed: Just form the triangle and acknowledge what's happening. That's enough. You don't have to complete all three steps when your nervous system is maxed out.

If you're autistic:

Do a sensory baseline check right now: On a scale of 1-10, how close are you to sensory overload? If you're above a 7, the Pivot won't work until you reduce sensory input first. Identify your sensory regulation tools (headphones, weighted blanket, dim lights, etc.) and use them before attempting cognitive techniques.

Practice body-based Acknowledge: Instead of labeling emotions, describe physical sensations. "My chest is tight. My hands are cold. Something feels wrong." That's valid Acknowledge even without emotion words.

Next time change is announced, try this adapted Adjust: "I don't have enough data to know if this is dangerous. Change feels threatening to my nervous system, but that doesn't mean the change itself is threatening. I can gather more information."

For all neurodivergent readers:

Pick one nervous system healing practice from this chapter and do it today. Not all of them—just one.

Bilateral stimulation while walking. Humming for 30 seconds. Gentle stretching. One practice, consistently, builds capacity over time.

6

When Life Hits Hard

"You can't stop the waves, but you can learn to surf."
— Jon Kabat-Zinn

Let's talk about the difference between spiraling and suffering.

Spiraling is when your brain catastrophizes about things that haven't happened yet. You imagine worst-case scenarios, convince yourself they're inevitable, and flood your body with stress hormones over futures that exist only in your mind.

The Perspective Pivot interrupts spiraling.

But suffering? Suffering is what happens when actual hard things occur. Job loss. Relationship endings. Health diagnoses. Death. Betrayal. Financial collapse.

The Pivot doesn't eliminate suffering. Nothing does.

But here's what it can do: it can help you navigate suffering without letting your spiral voice turn pain into catastrophe. It can help you feel what's actually happening without drowning in stories about what it means about your entire future.

This chapter is about using the Pivot when life genuinely hits hard. When you're not managing imagined disasters, but responding to real ones.

MY DAD'S CANCER DIAGNOSIS

I just found out my dad has prostate cancer.

I'm writing this in the middle of it, not after, not once I know how it ends, but right now, in the thick of not knowing. I don't know the stage, the prognosis, the treatment plan. I don't know if this is something we'll look back on as "that scary thing that turned out okay" or if it's the beginning of something harder.

And my brain, predictably, wants to fast-forward to every possible ending.

When I got the call, the world tilted slightly off its axis. It wasn't dramatic, no screaming, no collapsing. Just that quiet, suspended moment where your brain tries to decide if it's safe to fully register what it just heard.

I remember thinking: *Okay, breathe. Don't go to the worst place yet.*

But I did. My mind raced ahead to every what-if, every memory that suddenly felt weighted with finality, every version of loss I wasn't ready to imagine.

That's when I caught myself. Not because I'm good at this or because I've achieved some zen state where bad news doesn't hurt. I caught myself because I've practiced this exact moment a thousand times on smaller things, and the neural pathway was already there.

I was standing in my kitchen, phone still in my hand, and I could feel the choice point: spiral into suffering, or acknowledge the pain and stay present.

So I did the Pivot. Right there. In real time. While my hands were shaking.

Acknowledge: I'm terrified. My chest is tight. My mind is catastrophizing. I'm trying to solve a problem I don't have enough information to solve yet. This is fear. This is love. This is the weight of not knowing.

Adjust: I don't know how this ends. But "I don't know" is not the same as "worst case." Right now, in this moment, my dad is alive. Right now, there are doctors who know how to treat this. The story isn't "I'm losing my dad." The story is "I'm walking beside my dad through whatever comes next."

Align: I'm going to call him. Not later. Not when I feel more composed.

Right now. I'm going to tell him I love him without overthinking the words. I'm going to be present for this conversation instead of performing calm while spiraling internally.

I called him. I told him I loved him. My voice cracked. I didn't have wise words or reassuring platitudes. I just showed up, scared and human and there.

Here's what I need you to understand: the Perspective Pivot didn't fix this. It didn't erase the fear. It didn't give me certainty or peace. It didn't make me calm or okay.

It just gave me something to hold onto that wasn't
panic.

It let me stay connected to myself, to him, to the truth that both things can coexist: the ache of uncertainty and the gratitude of still having this moment.

THE PAIN VS. SUFFERING EQUATION

Buddhist psychology makes a distinction that changes everything once you understand it: Pain is inevitable. Suffering is what we add to pain.

Pain is: Your partner ended the relationship. Your body hurts. Someone you love died. You lost your job.

Suffering is: This means I'll be alone forever. This means my body is broken. This means I'll never recover. This means I'm unemployable.

Both are real. Both hurt. But they require different responses.

Pain requires presence, compassion, and allowing. Suffering requires the Pivot.

Your partner ends the relationship. The pain is real. Your heart is broken. You feel grief, loss, shock, anger. Let yourself feel that. Don't pivot away from actual emotion.

But then your spiral voice starts: "This proves I'm unlovable. I'll never find anyone else. There's something fundamentally wrong with me."

That's suffering. That's where the Pivot comes in. Not to stop you from grieving. To stop your spiral voice from turning heartbreak into identity assassination.

WHEN TO PIVOT, WHEN TO FEEL

Here's the guideline: If it's about what's happening right now, feel it. If it's about what it means about your entire future, pivot.

JOB LOSS

You just got laid off.

Pain to feel: Shock. Fear. Anger. Uncertainty. Grief for the identity and routine you just lost. Financial worry about the immediate future. Feel all of that. The Pivot doesn't bypass emotion. It protects you from the spiral that makes emotion unbearable.

Spiral to pivot: "I'll never find another job. I'm too old. My skills are outdated. I'm going to lose my house.

My career is over."

Acknowledge: "I just lost my job. I'm scared. My body is in shock. My spiral voice is catastrophizing my entire future based on one event that happened today."

Adjust: "I don't know what happens next. What do I actually know right now? I have savings for three months. I have skills that are valuable. I've navigated hard things before. Layoffs happen to competent people. This is one event, not my entire future."

Align: "Today, I'm going to let myself feel this.

Tomorrow, I'll start making a plan. Right now, I'm going to call someone who loves me. I'm going to let this be hard without making it mean I'm doomed."

You're not pivoting away from the legitimate fear and grief of job loss. You're pivoting away from the story that this one event defines your entire worth and future.

CRISIS-ADAPTED PIVOT: THE STRIPPED-DOWN VERSION

When you're in genuine crisis, the full three-step Pivot might be too much. Your cognitive resources are depleted. Your nervous system is maxed out. You can barely think straight.

Use the emergency version: Just Acknowledge.

That's it.

Form the triangle with your hands. Name what's true: "This is really hard. I'm overwhelmed. I don't know what to do. I'm scared."

Then take three breaths.

You don't have to Adjust. You don't have to Align.

Just acknowledge reality and breathe. That's enough in crisis.

Dr. Bessel van der Kolk's research on trauma shows that when your nervous system is in survival mode, complex cognitive tasks are inaccessible. But simple body-based practices (noticing breath, naming what's real, feeling your hands) remain accessible because they're governed by different neural pathways.

Crisis isn't the time to perform the Pivot perfectly.

It's the time to survive.

GRIEF AND THE PIVOT

Grief is its own category. It's not a crisis you solve or a spiral you interrupt. Grief is love with nowhere to go.

When someone you love dies, your spiral voice will absolutely show up. The Pivot can help with that. But it can't help with the grief itself.

What to pivot in grief:

"I should have called more often. If I'd just done something different, maybe this wouldn't have happened. I'll never be happy again. I can't survive this."

Catastrophic thoughts. Self-blame. Future predictions. Those are spirals.

What not to pivot in grief:

"I miss them so much it feels like my chest is caving in. I keep forgetting they're gone. I feel angry that they left. I feel guilty for feeling angry. I don't know who I am without them."

That's grief. That's the actual emotional processing of loss. Let that be.

Dr. David Kessler, who worked with Elisabeth Kübler-Ross on the five stages of grief, later added a sixth stage: meaning-making. Eventually, after feeling the grief, you'll start to make "meaning from the loss.

The Pivot can help make sure the meaning you make is honest, not catastrophic. "They died because I wasn't enough" is a catastrophic spiral. Pivot away from that. "They died because bodies are mortal, and death is part of being alive. I loved them. They loved me. That love still exists even though they don't" is meaning-making that honors reality.

ADDITIONAL CRISIS SCENARIOS

Financial Crisis

Money stress activates survival fear in ways few other things do. When you can't pay rent, when debt is crushing you, your nervous system goes into legitimate threat mode because financial insecurity is an actual threat.

What's real: You don't have enough money to cover this month's bills. What's spiral: "I'm a complete failure. I'll be homeless. I've ruined my entire life."

The Pivot: Acknowledge the real threat. Adjust by recognizing that financial crisis doesn't equal permanent poverty, being broke right now doesn't mean broke forever, and many people have recovered from worse.

Align by looking at exactly what you have and owe, researching resources for help, and handling this one piece at a time instead of drowning in shame.

Health Scare

You get test results that terrify you. A diagnosis you weren't expecting. Medical uncertainty is one of the most powerful spiral triggers that exists.

What's real: Something is happening with your body. You don't have complete information yet. What's spiral: "This is definitely cancer. I'm dying. My life is over."

The Pivot: Acknowledge that you're scared and don't have complete information yet. Adjust by remembering that scary symptoms don't always mean worst-case scenarios and you need actual medical information before you know what you're dealing with. Align by following up with your doctor, bringing someone to appointments, and letting this be uncertain without deciding the ending before you have facts.

Relationship Betrayal

When someone you trusted betrays you, when a relationship implodes, when you discover lies, your entire reality shatters. This is real trauma. Let yourself feel the anger, devastation, shock, grief, and rage.

What's real: This person lied to you. This relationship ended. Your trust was violated. What's spiral: "I'm too stupid to ever see truth. I'll never be able to trust anyone again. This is my fault for not being enough."

The Pivot: Acknowledge that you were betrayed and it's devastating, but your spiral voice is making this about your worth rather than their choices. Adjust by recognizing that their betrayal is about their choices, not your worth. Being betrayed doesn't mean you're unlovable. Align by letting yourself feel this, reaching out to people you trust, and giving yourself time to process before making permanent decisions.

Chronic Illness

If you're living with chronic illness, chronic pain, or disability, you're not pivoting through a temporary crisis. You're navigating ongoing reality. The Pivot isn't about positive thinking your way out of real symptoms. It's about preventing your spiral voice from taking real challenges and making them unbearable.

Feel the frustration of limitation. Pivot away from "I'll never get better. I'm a burden to everyone. My life is pointless." Your worth isn't determined by productivity. Having limits doesn't make you a burden. This is one hard day, not proof that all future days will be this hard.

WHEN MULTIPLE CRISES HIT SIMULTANEOUSLY

Sometimes life delivers five hard things at once. You lose your job while your parent is dying while your relationship is falling apart. Your nervous system is maxed out. You can barely function.

The Pivot in multiple crises: Don't try to pivot everything at once. Pick one. Today, you're pivoting about the job loss. The other crises exist, but you're not trying to cognitively process all five simultaneously. One crisis at a time. One pivot at a time.

Acknowledge that you're dealing with multiple genuine crises and can only handle one thing at a time. Adjust by recognizing that you don't have to solve everything today, you can prioritize, and bad timing isn't your fault. Align by handling the most urgent thing today and letting the rest wait.

THE TRAUMA-INFORMED PIVOT

If you have trauma history, crisis hits differently. Your nervous system doesn't just respond to the current crisis. It responds to every similar crisis from your past simultaneously.

Acknowledge that this situation is triggering your trauma response. You're not overreacting. You're responding to layers of pain. Adjust by reminding yourself that what happened before and what's happening now are not the same situation. You have more resources now. Align by using your trauma-informed coping tools, reaching out to your therapist, and reminding yourself that this is a trigger, not a recreation.

FOR MY NEURODIVERGENT READERS IN CRISIS

Crisis is harder when your nervous system is already running at capacity.

ADHD and crisis: Your executive function becomes nearly impossible. Don't try to manage crisis alone. You need external support, co-regulation, and someone else to help organize tasks and reduce decision fatigue.

Autism and crisis: Crisis disrupts routine, which disrupts your ability to regulate. Create as much predictability as possible in other areas. If your relationship is in crisis, keep your morning routine exactly the same. The parts of life that can stay predictable need to stay predictable to give your nervous system capacity.

The emergency signal: If you're neurodivergent and in crisis, you might need to explicitly tell people: "I'm in crisis mode. I need help." You might appear functional while internally drowning. Permission to unmask in crisis. Permission to ask for help.

WHEN THE PIVOT HELPS VS. WHEN YOU NEED MORE

The Pivot helps when your spiral voice is adding catastrophic layers to real pain, you're confusing pain with permanent meaning, you're stuck in shame spirals, or you're paralyzed by what might happen next.

The Pivot isn't enough when you're experiencing suicidal thoughts, you're dissociating or completely shut down, you've experienced acute trauma and need immediate support, you're in active danger, or you have clinical depression that makes basic functioning impossible.

In those situations, you need professional help. Call a therapist. Call a crisis line. Go to the emergency room. Get support. The Pivot is part of your mental health toolkit. It's not the only tool you need.

REBUILDING AFTER CRISIS

Here's what nobody tells you about crisis: the worst part often isn't the crisis itself. It's the aftermath. The crisis mobilizes you. Then the crisis ends, and you collapse. The adrenaline fades. You're left with reality and what it changed.

This is when your spiral voice comes back: "How do I rebuild? What if this happens again? What if I can't recover?"

Acknowledge that the crisis is over but you're not okay yet. You're exhausted and changed. Adjust by recognizing that recovery isn't linear. Having bad days doesn't mean you're not healing. Being changed by crisis doesn't mean you've failed. Align by taking one small step toward rebuilding today. Let recovery be messy and slow.

Crisis changes you. The Pivot helps you decide how. You can let crisis make you smaller and more afraid. Or you can let crisis show you that you're more resilient than you knew, more capable of surviving than your spiral voice admitted, more deserving of compassion than you believed.

Both are choices. The Pivot helps you make the second one.

In Chapter 7, we're going to narrow the focus to one specific area where crises and spirals show up constantly: work. Because your professional life is where you spend most of your waking hours, where your identity is often tied up, where spiraling can have real consequences.

How do you use the Pivot in workplace situations? That's next.

* * *

KEY TAKEAWAY

Pain is inevitable (loss, heartbreak, illness, betrayal, crisis). Suffering is what your spiral voice adds to pain through catastrophic stories about what it means about your entire future.

The Perspective Pivot doesn't eliminate suffering, but it helps you feel what's actually happening without drowning in narratives about permanent doom.

The guideline: if it's about what's happening right now, feel it. If it's about what it means about your entire future, pivot.

Use the crisis-adapted emergency version (just Acknowledge + three breaths) when you're overwhelmed. Don't pivot away from legitimate grief, fear, or anger.

Pivot away from the spiral voice using real pain as evidence of worthlessness. In multiple simultaneous crises, pick one to pivot about at a time.

In trauma activation, acknowledge that you're responding to layers of past and present. Crisis changes you. The Pivot helps you decide how, choosing resilience over permanent defeat.

We've covered how to use the Pivot when life delivers genuine crisis—loss, grief, betrayal, health scares. Now let's address the place where many of you spend most of your waking hours and experience your most frequent spirals: work.

* * *

TRY THIS

Think about something genuinely difficult you're facing right now—not an imagined worst-case scenario, but actual hard reality:

Separate pain from suffering:

- **What's the pain?** (The actual hard thing happening) Write it down in one sentence: "My pain is: ."

- **What's the suffering?** (The story your spiral voice is adding) Write down what your spiral voice is saying this pain means about you, your future, your worth: "My spiral voice is saying: ."

Now run just the suffering part through the Pivot:

- **ACKNOWLEDGE:** "This situation is genuinely hard. AND my spiral voice is adding catastrophic meaning on top of the actual pain. Both are happening."
- **ADJUST:** "The pain is real. But is the story my spiral voice is telling actually true? What evidence contradicts the catastrophic meaning? What would I tell a friend facing this same situation?"
- **ALIGN:** "Today, I'm going to let myself feel the actual pain without believing the catastrophic story. I'm going to take one small action that moves me forward, even if that action is just asking for help."

If you're too overwhelmed for all three steps: Just do the emergency version. Form the triangle with your hands. Say out loud or in your head: "This is really hard. I'm overwhelmed. I don't know what to do." Then take three slow breaths. That's enough. You acknowledged reality and stayed present with yourself. **That's the foundation everything else builds on.**

7

The Pivot At Work

"Your work is to discover your work and then with all your heart to give yourself to it."
— Buddha

You spend most of your waking life at work.

Which means most of your spiral triggers happen at work. The vague email from your boss. The meeting that goes sideways. The mistake you made that everyone saw. The project that's not going well. The colleague who seems cold. The performance review coming up. The presentation that terrifies you.

Your professional life is where spiraling has real consequences.

Spiraling at home might ruin your evening.

Spiraling at work can damage your reputation, torpedo your relationships, sabotage your performance, and derail your career.

This chapter is about using the Perspective Pivot in workplace situations where stakes are high, visibility is constant, and you don't always have the luxury of processing emotions before you have to respond.

THE UNIQUE CHALLENGES OF WORKPLACE SPIRALS

Work spirals are different from personal spirals in three critical ways.

First: Performance is visible and evaluated. When you spiral about your relationship at home, your partner might notice you're withdrawn, but they don't write a performance review about it. When you spiral about your work, your boss is watching. Your colleagues are forming opinions. Your mistakes are documented.

Second: You have to keep functioning while spiraling. At home, you can collapse on the couch. At work, you have deadlines, meetings, emails that need responses, presentations to deliver. You're expected to appear professional and competent while your nervous system is screaming.

Third: Professional identity is tied to self-worth.

For most people, work isn't just what you do. It's who you are. "I'm a teacher." "I'm an engineer." "I'm a manager." When work goes wrong, it doesn't just threaten your job. It threatens your identity.

All of this means workplace spirals require specific adaptations of the Pivot.

THE MOST COMMON WORKPLACE SPIRAL TRIGGERS

Trigger 1: The Vague Communication from Leadership
Subject: "Check in tomorrow at 2pm"

No context. No agenda. No explanation. Your spiral voice immediately generates seventeen disaster scenarios.

The Workplace Pivot:

Acknowledge (subtle triangle gesture at your desk): "I just got a vague meeting request. My stomach dropped. My spiral voice is catastrophizing. I'm making up stories before I have any actual information."

Adjust: "I literally cannot know what this meeting is about until it happens. My brain is guessing worst-case because that's what brains do with uncertainty. But guessing isn't knowing. What do I actually know about my performance? My last review was positive. My recent project got good feedback."

Align: "I'm going to finish my current task. If I have a specific question for the meeting, I'll send it in advance. Otherwise, I'm going to show up tomorrow prepared to listen and respond thoughtfully to whatever this is actually about."

The key workplace adaptation: Create closure before you have information. You can't know what the meeting is about. But you can decide how you'll show up to it. That decision creates a mental stopping point so you're not spiraling for the next 22 hours.

This builds on the Timeline Reality Check from Chapter 3—reminding your brain about actual timeframes versus catastrophic time collapse.

Trigger 2: The Public Mistake

You sent an email to the wrong distribution list. You gave wrong information in a meeting. You missed a deadline everyone was counting on. Everyone saw it.

Your spiral voice: "Everyone thinks I'm incompetent. They're all talking about this. I've lost all credibility. I'll never recover from this."

The Workplace Pivot:

Acknowledge: "I made a visible mistake. I'm mortified. My body is flooded with shame. My spiral voice is catastrophizing my entire professional reputation based on one error."

Adjust: "One mistake doesn't erase my track record. Everyone makes mistakes. How I handle this matters more than the mistake itself. People who are competent don't become incompetent because of one error." Evidence check: "Name three times I did something well recently. Name two times I saw colleagues make mistakes and it didn't destroy my opinion of them."

Align: "I'm going to acknowledge the mistake directly and fix it. I'm going to send a correction/apology/solution without excessive self-flagellation. Then I'm going to move forward. Dwelling in shame doesn't serve anyone."

The workplace-specific action: Clean acknowledgment, quick correction, move on. Don't hide the mistake. Don't spiral publicly. Acknowledge it, fix it, demonstrate you're still competent by moving forward professionally.

Trigger 3: The Upcoming Performance Review or High-Stakes Event

You have a performance review in two weeks. A big presentation next month. An important client meeting coming up. Your spiral voice starts rehearsing disaster weeks in advance.

The Workplace Pivot:

Acknowledge: "I have a high-stakes event coming up. I'm feeling anticipatory anxiety. My spiral voice is pre-living disaster scenarios that haven't happened yet. This is stealing my present moment to rehearse a catastrophic future."

Adjust: "Anxiety about performance is normal. It doesn't mean I'm unprepared or incapable. I've done presentations before. I've had reviews before. Feeling nervous doesn't predict failure. What evidence do I have that I can handle this? I've prepared. I know my material. Nervousness and competence can coexist."

Align: "I'm going to prepare appropriately without over-preparing. I'm going to practice my presentation three times, not thirty. I'm going to gather my performance data for the review, then stop obsessing. I'm going to set a 'worry window' (15 minutes tonight to think about this, then I'm done until tomorrow)."

The workplace-specific strategy: Bounded preparation. Preparation is useful. Rumination isn't. Decide in advance how much time you'll spend preparing, then stop. Create clear boundaries between productive planning and unproductive spiraling.

WORKPLACE PIVOT TECHNIQUES

At work, you can't always excuse yourself to do hand gestures in the bathroom. You're in a meeting. On a call. Sitting at your desk in an open office. Leading a presentation. You need invisible versions of the Pivot.

The Mental-Only Pivot

Acknowledge (no gesture, just internal dialogue): Silently name what's happening: "I'm activated right now. My spiral voice just kicked in. I'm feeling defensive /anxious/overwhelmed."

Adjust (while appearing to listen/think): Mentally ask: "What else could this mean? What am I assuming versus what do I actually know?"

Align (choose micro-action): Decide: "I'm going to ask a clarifying question" or "I'm going to take three breaths before responding" or "I'm going to table this reaction and revisit it later when I'm calmer."

Nobody needs to know you just interrupted a spiral. They just see you pausing thoughtfully before responding.

The Email Pivot

Work email is a spiral minefield. Tone is ambiguous. Intent is unclear. Your brain fills in gaps with worst-case interpretations.

Before you send an email written while spiraling:

Acknowledge: "I'm activated. I want to defend myself/explain/justify/correct. I'm about to send an email from an emotional place."

Adjust: "This email might feel urgent, but is it actually urgent? What would happen if I waited two hours to send this? Would I say this differently if I weren't activated?"

Align: "I'm going to save this as a draft. I'm going to wait [specific amount of time]. Then I'm going to re-read it before sending."

The 2-Hour Rule: Never send important emails within 2 hours of emotional activation. Draft it. Save it. Walk away. Come back with fresh eyes.

You'll catch things you would have regretted: defensive tone, unnecessary explanations, emotional language that doesn't serve you professionally.

The Meeting Pivot

You're in a meeting. Something happens that triggers you. Your boss criticizes your idea. A colleague takes credit for your work. Someone talks over you.

Acknowledge (internally): "I just got activated. I want to react immediately. My spiral voice is generating a defensive response."

Adjust (buy yourself time): Say out loud: "That's an interesting point. Let me think about that for a moment." Or: "Can you say more about that?" Or: "I want to make sure I understand what you're asking."

You're creating a 30-second pause so your prefrontal cortex can catch up to your amygdala.

Align (respond from intention, not reaction): Now that you've paused, you can respond thoughtfully instead of defensively. "I hear your concern about X. Here's the data that informed my approach." "I appreciate that feedback. I'll consider how to adjust the plan."

The workplace-specific skill: The strategic pause. "Let me think about that" buys you time to pivot without anyone knowing you're doing it.

IMPOSTER SYNDROME AND THE PIVOT

Imposter syndrome is a specific type of workplace spiral: "I don't deserve to be here. Everyone else is more qualified. I'm going to be exposed as a fraud."

Acknowledge: "I'm experiencing imposter syndrome. The feeling of being a fraud doesn't mean I am one."

Adjust: "What's the actual evidence of my competence? I was hired because I demonstrated skills. I've completed projects successfully. People seek my input. The Imposter Paradox: the fact that I'm worried about being incompetent is evidence I care about doing well. Actual incompetent people rarely worry about this."

Align: "I'm going to act as if I belong here, because I do. I'm going to contribute my ideas even though I feel uncertain. I'm going to let my work speak instead of my anxiety."

The workplace-specific reframe: Imposter syndrome often hits competent people in stretch roles. If you never feel like an imposter, you're probably not challenging yourself enough.

THE FEEDBACK PIVOT

Receiving critical feedback triggers spiraling faster than almost anything else at work. Your boss says: "I'd like to see improvement in how you communicate with stakeholders." Your spiral voice hears: "You're terrible at communication. You're failing. You're about to get fired."

Quick Pivot for Feedback:

Acknowledge: This is feedback about one specific skill, not a referendum on my entire competence

Adjust: My boss wouldn't give me feedback on improving if they thought I was hopeless. Feedback is information, not condemnation

Align: Ask for specifics: "Can you give me an example of what effective stakeholder communication would look like?" "What's one thing I could change this week that would show improvement?"

Specific feedback is easier to act on than vague criticism, and asking for it demonstrates you're taking it seriously rather than spiraling.

FOR MY NEURODIVERGENT READERS AT WORK

Workplace demands hit neurodivergent brains differently.

ADHD at work: Executive function challenges mean task initiation, organization, and time management are constant struggles. You might be brilliant at the creative or analytical parts of your job but terrible at the administrative parts.

When you spiral about being "lazy" or "disorganized," remember: Executive dysfunction isn't a character flaw. It's a neurological difference.

Adjust: "I'm not lazy. My executive function is impaired. I need external structure and accountability. Needing support isn't the same as being incompetent."

Align: "I'm going to ask for accommodations that help me work with my brain, not against it. Body doubling, external deadlines, clear priorities. I'm going to stop apologizing for needing structure."

Autism at work: Social communication expectations, unclear feedback, ambiguous instructions, and sensory environments not designed for your neurology create constant overwhelm.

When you spiral about "not fitting in" or "being difficult," remember: The workplace wasn't designed for your brain. That's a design problem, not a you problem.

Adjust: "I'm not bad at my job because I need written instructions instead of verbal ones. I'm not unprofessional because I need direct feedback instead of hints. I'm working in a system not built for my neurology."

Align: "I'm going to advocate for what I need. Clear expectations. Written communication. Sensory accommodations. I'm going to stop masking at the cost of my capacity."

THE BOUNDARY BETWEEN WORK AND IDENTITY

Here's the most important workplace Pivot of all: Your job is what you do. It's not who you are.

When work spirals threaten your identity, you need to pivot back to this truth:

Acknowledge: "My worth as a human isn't determined by my professional success. My job performance doesn't define my value as a person."

Adjust: "I can care about doing well at work without making work my entire identity. I can want to succeed professionally without believing failure would make me worthless. Separating my job from my worth doesn't mean I don't care. It means I'm sustainable."

Align: "I'm going to invest in my life outside of work. Relationships. Hobbies. Rest. Things that remind me I'm more than my job title."

The workplace-specific wisdom: Professional competence and human worth are separate categories. You can be struggling at work and still be a valuable human being. You can be succeeding at work and still need to develop other parts of yourself. Work is part of your life. It's not the entirety of your life.

In Chapter 8, we're going to bring everything together, how to build what I call "spiral immunity," where triggers lose their power over time, where you develop such skill at pivoting that spiraling becomes less frequent, less intense, and shorter-lived.

You're learning to navigate spirals. Chapter 8 teaches you how to make them nearly obsolete.

* * *

KEY TAKEAWAY

Workplace spirals are uniquely challenging because performance is visible and evaluated, you must keep functioning while activated, and professional identity is often tied to self-worth.

The most common workplace triggers (vague communications, public mistakes, and high-stakes events) each require specific Pivot adaptations.

At work, you need both the full Pivot when you have privacy and the invisible mental-only version when you're in meetings or public spaces.

The 2-Hour Rule (never send important emails within 2 hours of activation) and strategic pauses ("let me think about that") buy you time to pivot without anyone knowing.

Imposter syndrome and critical feedback are specific workplace spirals that respond to evidence-based Adjusting.

For neurodivergent professionals, workplace struggles often aren't about competence but about working in systems not designed for your neurology.

The most important workplace Pivot: your job is what you do, not who you are. Professional performance and human worth are separate categories.

* * *

TRY THIS

Identify your biggest workplace spiral trigger from the past month. Write it down specifically: "The situation was:."

Now run it through the Workplace Pivot:

1. **ACKNOWLEDGE:** What did you feel when it happened? What did your spiral voice immediately say? Write the catastrophic narrative your brain generated: "My spiral voice said: ."

2. **ADJUST - Evidence Check:** What actual evidence did you have versus what were you assuming? Write down three facts that contradict your spiral voice's interpretation.

3. **ADJUST - Workplace Reframe:** If a colleague experienced this exact situation and came to you for perspective, what would you tell them? Often we can see clearly for others what we can't see for ourselves.

4. **ALIGN - Professional Action:** What's one action that would have reflected competence and professionalism in that moment? Write it down: "Next time this happens, I will: ."

Practice the Invisible Pivot: Next time you're in a meeting and feel yourself getting activated, try the mental-only version. Don't excuse yourself. Don't make hand gestures. Just internally run through Acknowledge-Adjust-Align while maintaining professional composure externally. Notice that you can pivot completely invisibly while appearing thoughtful and composed to others.

Create your 2-Hour Email Draft folder: Right now, create a "Drafts-Wait" folder in your email. Next time you write an email while activated, save it there instead of sending. Set a 2-hour timer. When it goes off, re-read with fresh eyes before sending. Notice how different the email feels after your nervous system has settled.

IV

MOVING FORWARD

8

From Practice To Instinct

"We cannot become what we want by remaining what we are."
— Max DePree

Here's what nobody tells you about mastering the Perspective **Pivot:** the goal isn't to get so good at interrupting spirals that you're constantly using the technique.

The goal is to need it less and less because spirals stop forming in the first place.

That's spiral immunity.

Not because anxiety disappears. Not because triggers stop happening. But because your nervous system learns, through hundreds of successful pivots, that uncertainty doesn't equal danger.

Your brain's threat detection system recalibrates. The triggers that used to send you into three-day spirals now register as minor blips. The situations that used to hijack you completely now activate you briefly before your system naturally regulates.

You're not working harder to manage spirals.

You're experiencing fewer spirals to manage.

This chapter is about what happens after you've been practicing the Pivot for months. How transformation deepens. How skills become instincts.

125

How you build the kind of resilience that doesn't require constant effort to maintain.

WHAT SPIRAL IMMUNITY ACTUALLY LOOKS LIKE

Let me be clear about what this isn't.

Spiral immunity doesn't mean you never get anxious. It doesn't mean triggers don't activate you. It doesn't mean uncertainty feels comfortable.

You're still human. You still have a nervous system wired for survival.

But here's what changes:

The activation window shortens (three days becomes thirty minutes)

The intensity decreases (drowning becomes treading water)

Recovery happens faster (hours instead of weeks)

Triggers lose their predictive power (you stop believing every worst-case thought)

The spiral voice becomes background noise (it still speaks, but you don't automatically believe it)

Think of it like this: you used to be a swimmer who panicked every time a wave came. Now you're a swimmer who sees the wave coming, adjusts your stroke, and keeps swimming. The waves didn't stop. You got better at navigating them.

THE THREE PHASES OF SPIRAL IMMUNITY

Building immunity happens in three distinct phases. Most people don't realize they're progressing because the changes are gradual.

Phase 1: Reactive Mastery (Months 1-3)

You're getting good at using the Pivot when you remember to use it. You still spiral regularly. But now you catch yourself mid-spiral and pivot back. Sometimes it takes hours to remember. Sometimes minutes.

Occasionally, you catch it within seconds.

You're building the neural pathway. Every time you successfully pivot, you're strengthening the connection between trigger and regulation response.

What it feels like: Exhausting. You're hypervigilant about spirals because you're still in conscious competence. You have to deliberately remember to use the technique.

Progress markers: You catch yourself spiraling within the same day instead of days later. You recognize your specific spiral patterns. The Pivot works more often than it doesn't. Other people notice you're recovering from setbacks faster.

Phase 2: Preventive Awareness (Months 3-6)

You're starting to catch triggers before they become full spirals. You notice the moment your nervous system activates. You feel the stomach drop, the chest tightening, the thought pattern starting. And before the catastrophic narrative fully forms, you pivot.

The connection between activation and pivot response is getting automated. Your interoceptive awareness is sharpening. You're catching the physical activation that precedes catastrophic thinking.

What it feels like: Empowering. You're preventing spirals rather than just managing them. You're seeing evidence that you can navigate uncertainty skillfully.

Progress markers: You notice body activation before catastrophic thoughts fully form. Certain triggers that used to cause major spirals now barely register. You can use the Pivot in high-pressure situations. Your baseline anxiety is lower.

Phase 3: Embodied Resilience (Months 6+)

The Pivot becomes so automatic that you barely notice you're doing it. A trigger happens. Your nervous system does its job, notices potential threat, activates slightly.

And before you even consciously register it, you've already generated alternative interpretations and chosen aligned action.

The new response pattern has become your default. The neural pathway from trigger to catastrophe is weaker. The pathway from trigger to perspective is stronger because you've reinforced it hundreds of times.

What it feels like: Natural. Like breathing. You don't think about pivoting, you just do it. And increasingly, you don't even need to because spirals don't form.

Progress markers: You realize days later that something happened that used to trigger you and you barely noticed. Friends comment that you seem calmer, more grounded, less reactive. Setbacks that used to devastate you now just happen, and you handle them. You have capacity to support others because you're not drowning in your own spirals.

THE COMPOUND EFFECT OF MICRO-PIVOTS

Here's something most people miss: transformation doesn't come from the big dramatic pivots. It comes from the thousands of tiny ones you barely notice.

You're standing in line at the coffee shop. Someone cuts in front of you. Old you would have spiraled: "People are so rude. Nobody respects me. Why does this always happen to me?"

New you notices the irritation, thinks "that was rude, and also I don't know what's going on in their day," and returns attention to your order.

That micro-pivot took three seconds. You might not even consciously register it as using the technique. But your brain registered it. Neural pathway strengthened.

Evidence accumulated: I can handle minor frustrations without catastrophizing.

You do this twenty times a day. Small irritations. Minor disappointments. Tiny uncertainties. Each micro-pivot is a deposit in your resilience account.

Over months, those deposits compound. You're not just better at handling big crises. You're fundamentally more regulated at baseline because you're not constantly being drained by micro-spirals.

WHAT MASTERY ACTUALLY LOOKS LIKE

People think mastery means perfection. It doesn't.

Mastery means you fail less often, recover faster, and learn from each setback.

Here's what mastery actually looks like:

You still spiral sometimes. But when you do, you notice within minutes instead of hours. You pivot back quickly. You don't beat yourself up for spiraling, you treat it as data.

You have bad days. But bad days don't turn into bad weeks. You can have a hard morning and a decent afternoon because you're not carrying activation forward.

You make mistakes. But mistakes don't trigger identity crises. You can acknowledge "I messed up" without spiraling into "I'm a mess."

You encounter genuine crises. But you don't add suffering on top of pain. You feel the hard thing without letting your spiral voice turn it into evidence of permanent doom.

Mastery is skilled navigation, not perfect avoidance.

THE MAINTENANCE PHASE: KEEPING WHAT YOU'VE BUILT

Once you've built spiral immunity, you don't need to practice the Pivot daily like you did in the beginning.

But you do need maintenance.

Think of it like physical fitness. You can't work out intensely for six months, then stop completely and expect to maintain strength. But you don't need to maintain the same intensity you needed to build strength.

Pivot maintenance looks like:

Weekly check-ins: Once a week, run through a retrospective pivot on something from the past week. Keeps the pathway active.

Crisis refreshers: When life delivers genuine stress (job change, relationship shift, health issue, major life transition) return to daily practice temporarily. You're not starting over, you're reinforcing what you built.

Continued body-based practices: The somatic regulation tools from Chapter 5 (bilateral stimulation, humming, gentle movement, weighted pressure) continue to support your nervous system even when you're not actively spiraling.

Environmental adjustments: As you gain clarity about your triggers, you can sometimes change environments instead of just managing reactions.

You built the skill. Now you're sustaining it.

WHEN SPIRAL IMMUNITY REVEALS DEEPER WORK

Here's something that happens to many people after months of practicing the Pivot: the everyday spirals quiet down. And underneath them, you discover deeper patterns that were always there but were hidden by the noise.

Maybe you realize your spiraling about work was actually about needing your father's approval. Maybe you notice that your catastrophic thinking about relationships always involves abandonment, and you trace it back to childhood attachment wounds. Maybe you see that your constant need to be productive is covering up a belief that rest equals worthlessness.

The Pivot quieted the symptoms. Now you can see the root.

This is where therapy becomes valuable if you haven't already engaged with it. The Pivot gives you real-time regulation. Therapy helps you process the deeper material. They work beautifully together.

Don't see this as the Pivot failing. See it as the Pivot succeeding so well that it created space for deeper work.

SPIRAL IMMUNITY AND RELATIONSHIPS

As you build spiral immunity, your relationships change.

You stop projecting your catastrophic interpretations onto other people's behavior. You can hear feedback without immediately spiraling into shame.

You can handle conflict without assuming the relationship is ending. You become a more regulated presence for others.

But here's what also happens: as you regulate, you notice dysregulation in others more clearly. People who used to feel "normal" now feel draining. Relationships that used to work now feel unbalanced. Dynamics you tolerated now feel unacceptable.

This isn't judgment. It's clarity. When you're chronically dysregulated, you can't tell the difference between your chaos and someone else's. When you regulate, you can.

Some relationships deepen. The people who were safe all along become even more precious. Some relationships end. The people who needed you to stay small or anxious can't adjust to your growth.

Both are part of transformation.

THE IDENTITY SHIFT

The deepest change isn't behavioral. It's identity.

You used to be someone who spiraled constantly.

Someone whose anxiety ran the show. Someone who couldn't trust their own nervous system.

Through thousands of pivots, you become someone different. Someone who can handle uncertainty. Someone whose worth isn't determined by catastrophic thoughts. Someone who recovers quickly from setbacks.

You don't think about it consciously. You just notice one day that you responded to a trigger completely differently than you would have six months ago.

You're not trying to be different. You are different.

The spiral voice is still there sometimes. But it's not you anymore. It's just noise in the background that you've learned not to take personally.

TEACHING OTHERS THE PIVOT

At some point in your journey, someone will notice your transformation. "You seem calmer." "How do you handle stress so well?" "What changed for you?"

You'll have the opportunity to teach them the
Pivot.

Here's what I've learned about teaching this work to others:

Don't explain it all at once. Start with the Triple-A Hand Hack. Show them the physical gestures. Let them experience it.

Use recent examples from their life. "Remember yesterday when you were spiraling about that email? Let's run it through the Pivot together."

Meet them where they are. Some people need the neuroscience. Others just need the technique. Adapt.

Share your struggles, not just your successes.

Show them the messy middle. That's what makes it real.

Remember: you can't make someone ready. They have to hit their own bottom with spiraling. You can offer the tool. You can't make them use it.

WHEN LIFE TESTS YOUR IMMUNITY

You'll have moments where you think you've lost everything you built.

A major life crisis hits. Grief overwhelms you. Trauma gets triggered. Health collapses. Relationship ends. Job disappears.

You spiral hard. Maybe for days. And you think: "I'm back to square one. All that practice was for nothing."

That's not true.

Spiral immunity doesn't mean you never spiral again. It means you notice you're spiraling faster, you have tools to navigate it even in crisis, you recover more quickly than you would have before, and you don't add layers of shame about spiraling on top of the actual hard thing.

You're allowed to fall apart during genuine crisis.

That's not regression. That's being human.

What's different is that you don't stay apart as long. You have a way back.

FOR MY NEURODIVERGENT READERS: IMMUNITY LOOKS DIFFERENT

If you're neurodivergent, your spiral immunity won't look like neurotypical immunity.

Your baseline activation will likely always be higher because you're navigating a world not designed for your neurology. Your sensory sensitivities won't disappear. Your executive function won't become neurotypical. Your RSD won't vanish. Your need for predictability won't evaporate.

But here's what changes:

You start seeing your brain as different, not defective.

You get better at recognizing when spiraling is about the situation versus when it's about sensory overload, executive dysfunction, or other neurodivergent factors.

You develop accommodations and environments that work with your neurology instead of against it.

You stop masking as much because you realize masking was keeping you in chronic activation.

Your immunity isn't "acting more neurotypical." It's working more skillfully with your actual neurology.

THE REVOLUTION CONTINUES

You started this book spiraling regularly, convinced your anxiety was just who you are.

You learned that spiraling is a pattern, not a personality. A habit, not an identity.

You discovered the three-second window between trigger and catastrophe.

You practiced Acknowledge, Adjust, Align until it became second nature. You built the physical anchors that work when thinking fails. You adapted the technique for your specific neurology. You navigated crisis without letting spiral voice turn pain into suffering. You used the Pivot at work, in relationships, in grief, in growth. And now you're building immunity.

Not immunity from life's challenges. Not immunity from pain or uncertainty.

Immunity from the spiral voice's ability to hijack you.

You're becoming someone who can hold space for hard things without adding catastrophic layers. Someone who can feel uncertain without deciding it means disaster. Someone who can be anxious and capable simultaneously.

That's the revolution.

Not the elimination of anxiety. The transformation of your relationship with it.

The spirals will still come. Triggers will still activate you. Hard things will still be hard.

But you are not the same person who opened this book.

You have something now that you didn't have before — not a cure, not a guarantee, not a life without anxiety. Something more durable than any of those things.

You have three seconds.

And in those three seconds, you have everything: the ability to catch the story before it becomes a verdict. The skill to interrupt the spiral before it steals the day. The proof, earned through hundreds of imperfect practice reps, that you are more capable of navigating uncertainty than your spiral voice will ever admit.

The revolution was never about silence. It was never about calm.

It was always about choice.

You have yours.

* * *

KEY TAKEAWAY

Spiral immunity isn't about never getting anxious. It's about triggers losing their power to hijack you completely.

It develops in three phases:

- *Reactive Mastery* (months 1-3) where you catch spirals mid-occurrence;
- *Preventive Awareness* (months 3-6) where you notice triggers before spirals fully form;
- *Embodied Resilience* (months 6+) where pivoting becomes so automatic you barely notice you're doing it.

Transformation comes not from dramatic pivots but from thousands of micro-pivots compounding over time.

Mastery looks like failing less often, recovering faster, and learning from setbacks (skilled navigation, not perfect avoidance).

Maintenance requires weekly check-ins and crisis refreshers, not daily practice forever. As everyday spirals quiet down, deeper patterns may emerge. The Pivot created space for deeper therapeutic work. Spiral immunity is measured in months and years, and for neurodivergent brains, it looks like working skillfully with your neurology, not trying to become neurotypical.

* * *

TRY THIS

Assess your current phase of spiral immunity:

Phase 1 Check (Reactive Mastery):

- How quickly do you notice when you're spiraling? (Same day? Within hours? Within minutes?)
- Can you name your three most common spiral triggers?
- Does the Pivot work more often than it fails when you remember to use it?

Phase 2 Check (Preventive Awareness):

- Can you catch the body activation before catastrophic thoughts fully form?
- Are there triggers that used to cause major spirals that now barely register?
- Can you use the Pivot in public/high-pressure situations, not just in private?

Phase 3 Check (Embodied Resilience):

- Do you sometimes realize days later that something happened that used to trigger you and you barely noticed?
- Have others commented that you seem calmer or more grounded?
- Can you handle setbacks without extended spiraling?

Mark where you are. This is your baseline.

Now, create your maintenance plan:
  If you're in Phase 1 or 2, keep daily practice going.
  You're still building the pathway.

* * *

The Perspective Pivot

Flip your perspective. Change everything.

Appendix A: The Perspective Pivot Quick Reference Guide

THE CORE FRAMEWORK

ACKNOWLEDGE Name what's happening without judgment. "I'm having the thoughtthat…" "I'm noticingI feel…" "My brain is telling me…" "My body feels…"

ADJUST Ask: "What else could be true?" Generateat least 2-3 alternative perspectives Don't judge them as "right" or "wrong"—just create options Look for evidence, not just feelings Consider what you'd tell a friend in this situation

ALIGN Take one small action that moves you forward. Ask: "What's the smallest next thing I can do right now?" Choose based on your values, not your fear Do it. Then reassess. Action can be tiny—standing up counts

THE TRIPLE-A HAND HACK

- **Step 1: ACKNOWLEDGE** Bring the tips of your thumbs and index fingers together to form a triangle (an "A" shape).
- **Step 2: ADJUST** Keep your index fingers touching, but separate your thumbs, breaking the triangle apart.
- **Step 3: ALIGN** Rotate your hands so your index fingers point straight

ahead, touching tip to tip, with your thumbs resting on top.

Use this:

- Before high-stakes moments(presentations, difficult conversations)
- When you feel a spiral starting
- As a physical anchor to bring you back to the present
- Anytime you need a 3-second reset
- When cognitive techniques alone aren't accessible

THE ONE-HANDED VERSION

Hand Position: Touch your thumb and index fingertips together on one hand, forming a small triangle. Other fingers relaxed.

Use this discreet version during meetings, in public, while driving, or as a quick "micro-pivot" throughout your day.

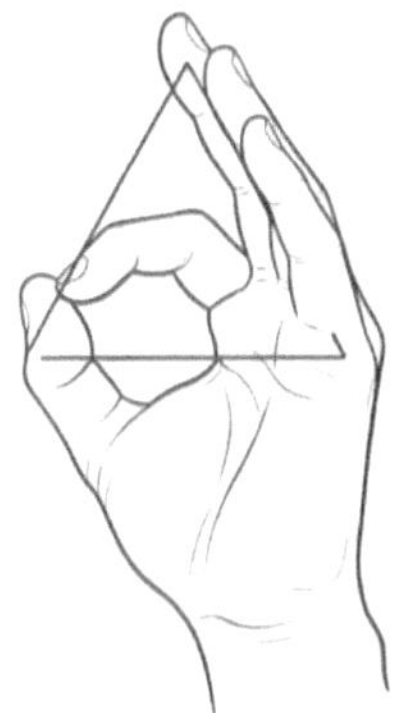

Bring thumb and index finger tips together, creating a small triangle. Remaining fingers gently curved.

Figure 6: One-Handed Hand Hack - Discreet version for public settings

THE 60-SECOND EMERGENCY PIVOT

0-20 seconds: ACKNOWLEDGE Say out loud or write: "I am spiraling about [specific thing]. My body feels [physical sensation]. This is anxiety, not reality."

20-40 seconds: ADJUST Ask: "What's one thing I know for sure right now that's actually okay?" (Example: I'm safe. I'm breathing. I have people who care about me. This feeling will pass.)

40-60 seconds: ALIGN Do ONE thing: Drink water, text one person, stand up and move, put your hand on your chest, and take three breaths.

COMMON SPIRAL TYPES & PIVOT SCRIPTS

Type 1: Catastrophic Thinking Spiral:

Everything is falling apart. This is a disaster. I can't handle this.

- **Acknowledge:** I'm catastrophizing. My brain is jumping to worst-case scenarios. My body is [physical sensation]. This is my threat response activating.
- **Adjust:** What's actually happening right now, versus what I'm imagining might happen? Have my worst-case predictions come true before? What evidence contradicts this catastrophic story?
- **Align:** What's one thing I can do right now to address the actual situation (not the imagined catastrophe)?

Type 2: Comparison Spiral:

Everyone else has it together. I'm the only one struggling. I'm so far behind.

- **Acknowledge:** I'm comparing my behind-the-scenes to everyone else's highlight reel. I'm measuring my worth against other people's visible success.

- **Adjust:** What if everyone is struggling but just not broadcasting it? What if "behind" is subjective, and I'm actually making progress at my own pace? What if my timeline doesn't need to match theirs?
- **Align:** What's one thing I accomplished today/this week that proves I'm moving forward, even if it doesn't look like someone else's version?

Type 3: Imposter Syndrome Spiral:

I don't deserve to be here. I'm a fraud. Eventually, everyone will figure out I don't know what I'm doing.

- **Acknowledge:** I'm having imposter thoughts. This is my brain's threat response to success or visibility. The fact that I'm worried about competence often means I care about doing well.
- **Adjust:** What evidence do I have that I WAS chosen/hired/invited for legitimate reasons? What skills do I actually possess? Would I call a colleague with my exact credentials a fraud?
- **Align:** Instead of trying to "prove" I belong, what if I just focus on doing my job well today?

Type 4: Rumination About Past Mistakes Spiral:

I can't believe I said/did that. Everyone thinks I'm [stupid/unprofessional/incompetent]. This will define me forever.

- **Acknowledge:** I'm replaying a past event and adding catastrophic meaning to it. My brain is using one data point to create a permanent identity story.
- **Adjust:** How much do I actually remember about other people's mistakes? Do I define them by their worst moments? What if this is one data point, not my entire identity? What would I tell a friend who

made the same mistake?

- **Align:** What's one thing I can do right now that moves me forward instead of keeping me stuck in the past? (Apologize if needed, learn the lesson, then close the loop.)

Type 5: Anticipatory Anxiety Spiral:

What if I fail?What if they hate it? What if I embarrass myself? What if everything goes wrong?

- **Acknowledge:** I'm anxiety-projecting into the future. My brain is trying to prepare for threats that haven't happened and might never happen.
- **Adjust:** What if it goes well? What if I'm more prepared than I think? What if "failure" isn't as catastrophic as my brain is predicting? What evidence do I have of past resilience?
- **Align:** What's one thing I can do right now to prepare, so I feel more in control of the outcome? Then I'm going to set boundaries around worrying and focus on what's actually in front of me.

Type 6: Rejection Sensitivity Spiral:

They didn't respond. They hate me. I did something wrong. They're mad at me.

- **Acknowledge:** I'm interpreting silence/delayed response as rejection. My brain is filling in blanks with worst-case assumptions.
- **Adjust:** What are three non-rejection reasons they might not have responded? (Busy, didn't see it, dealing with their own stuff, forgot, tech issues, their response isn't actually required)
- **Align:** Instead of spiraling about their response, what do I need right now to feel okay regardless of their timeline?

CRISIS PIVOT SCRIPT

Crisis ACKNOWLEDGE: Narrate what's actually happening right now (facts only, no interpretation). "I just got difficult news. I'm sitting on my couch. My chest is tight. It's 3 PM. I'm safe in this moment."

Crisis ADJUST: Ask:"What do I need right now to get 1% more stable?" (Not "How do I solve this?" Just: Water?
  Movement? Calling someone?Crying? Getting outside?)

Crisis ALIGN: Do the smallest possible thing directly in front of you. Respond to one text. Drink water. Take a shower. Feed yourself. One thing.

WORKPLACE PIVOT SCRIPTS

Before A High-Stakes Meeting:

- **Acknowledge:** I'm nervous. My stomach is tight. I'm worried about [specific thing].
- **Adjust:** I've prepared. I know my material. Nerves don't mean I'm unprepared—they mean I care. What evidence do I have that I can handle this?
- **Align:** I'm going to review my opening point one more time, then take three slow breaths. Then I'm walking in and doing my job.

After A Difficult Interaction:

- **Acknowledge:** That was uncomfortable. I'm replaying it and adding negative meaning. My brain is scanning for what I did wrong.
- **Adjust:** What's the most neutral interpretation of what happened? What

if it wasn't as bad as my brain is making it? What would an objective observer say?

- **Align:** I'm going to send a brief follow-up if needed, then focus on a different task to interrupt the rumination.

When You Make A Visible Mistake:

- **Acknowledge:** I made a mistake. I'm feeling [embarrassed/panicked/exposed]. My brain is catastrophizing about what this means about me.
- **Adjust:** What if everyone makes mistakes, and this is just data, not identity? What if people are far less focused on my error than I think? What would I tell someone else who made this same mistake?
- **Align:** I'm going to address it once (apologize/fix it/acknowledge it), then move on. Dwelling doesn't undo it.

The 2-Hour Email Rule:

If an email makes you spiral, close it. Use the Pivot. Wait 2 hours. Then respond.

NEURODIVERGENT ADAPTATIONS

ADHD Pivots:

External reminders: Set alarms, sticky notes, or visual cues. Body-first pivots: Move first, think second—jump,

shake, walk before attempting cognitive Adjust

Voice-record your Pivots if writing feels like too much friction

Time-blind adjustments: Use "How would I think about this tomorrow?" instead of abstract timelines

Autism Pivots:

Script your common spirals in advance (use templates from this guide)

Write out your Pivot if speaking it feels too demanding

Sensory regulation before cognitive Pivot: weighted pressure, specific textures, noise-canceling

Remove eye contact requirement—you can Pivot while looking away, stimming, or lying down

RSD (Rejection Sensitive Dysphoria) Pivot:

- **Acknowledge:** This is RSD. The pain I'm feeling is neurological amplification, not evidence.
- **Adjust:** What if this isn't actually rejection? What

If my brain is adding rejection meaning where none exists?

- **Align:** I'm going to regulate my nervous system first (walk, weighted blanket, safe person), then reassess.

NERVOUS SYSTEM REGULATION TOOLS

Quick Regulation (when dysregulated):

- *Bilateral stimulation:* Walk, tap knees alternately, butterfly hug
- *Humming or singing:* Activates vagus nerve
- *Weighted pressure:* Weighted blanket, tight hug, compression clothing
- *Movement:* Shake your body, do jumping jacks, dance
- *Cold water:* Splash face, drink cold water
- *Grounding:* 5-4-3-2-1 (name 5 things you see, 4 you hear, 3 you feel, 2 you smell, 1 you taste)

Daily Capacity-Building:

- *Co-regulation:* Time with calm, safe people or pets
- *Somatic practices:* Gentle yoga, tai chi, stretching
- *Consistent routine:* Predictable daily rhythms

- *Sensory diet:* Regular sensory input tailored to your needs
- *Unmasking:* Spaces where you can be yourself without performing

THE DAILY PIVOT PRACTICE

Morning Practice (5 Minutes):

- **Acknowledge your current state:** "I'm feeling [rested/anxious/groggy/calm/activated]."
- **Adjust one yesterday thought:** "Yesterday I thought: [unhelpful thought]. What else could be true: [alternative perspective]."
- **Align with today's intention:** "Today I will [one specific action that aligns with who I want to be]."

Evening Review (5 Minutes):

- **Name today's spirals: "I spiraled** about [X] and [Y]."
- **Identify the triggers:** "[X] was triggered by [specific situation/person/thought]."
- **Note what helped:** "What worked: [tool I used].

What didn't:[pattern I fell into]. Tomorrow I'll try: [adjustment]."

TROUBLESHOOTING GUIDE

"I can't think of alternative perspectives in Adjust."

Try these prompts:

- If my best friend were in this situation, what would I tell them?
- What would I think about this tomorrow? Next week? Next year?
- What's the most boring, neutral explanation for what happened?
- What would someone who loves me say about this?

- What would my therapist/mentor/trusted person say?
- What evidence exists that contradicts my catastrophic thought?

"The Pivot isn't working."

The most common reason is that you're reaching for it too late — after the spiral is already running at full speed. The Pivot is most effective in the early seconds, before your brain has locked onto the catastrophic story. If you're using it mid-flood, try just Acknowledge first. Form the triangle, name what's happening, take one breath. Don't force Adjust until your nervous system has a little more space. Also check: are you treating Adjust as positive thinking? It isn't. You're generating options, not choosing "happy thoughts." And if the Pivot consistently isn't working despite sincere practice, that may be a signal that there's deeper work to do — with a therapist, not just a tool.

"I keep forgetting to use it."

This is the most normal thing in the world and it's not a character flaw — it's how skill development works. Your brain has decades of practice spiraling. The Pivot has weeks. The solution isn't to try harder to remember. It's to engineer your environment so the reminder is external, not internal. Phone alarms at your highest-risk times. A sticky note on your bathroom mirror. The hand gesture practiced every morning so your hands know it before your brain needs it. Tell one person you're practicing and ask them to check in. The forgetting isn't failure. It's the gap the practice is closing.

MASTERY TIMELINE

- **Stage 1: Recognition (Weeks 1-4)** You catch spirals hours or days after they happen.
- **Stage 2: Interruption (Weeks 5-12)** You catch spirals mid-spin and remember to use the Pivot.
- **Stage 3: Prevention (Weeks 13-24)** You recognize triggers before the

spiral fully activates.

- **Stage 4: Integration (6+ months)** The Pivot is automatic—you think this way now.

KEY REMINDERS

- The Pivot doesn't prevent spiraling—it shortens recovery time
- You will forget to use it sometimes. That's normal, not failure.
- Practice on small spirals when stakes are low, so it's available when stakes are high
- Adjust is NOT forced positivity—it's generating options, not choosing "happy thoughts."
- Align is about action, not perfection. Small steps count.
- Your spiral patterns have decades of practice. The Pivot has weeks. Be patient.
- Neurodivergent brains need adaptations. You're not doing it wrong.
- If crisis overwhelms the Pivot, get professional support. Tools work together.
- Integration takes 6+ months. You're building new neural pathways.
- Nervous system regulation before cognitive techniques

CRISIS RESOURCES

988 Suicide & Crisis Lifeline (US): Call or text 988 SAMHSA National Helpline: 1-800-662-4357 Crisis Text Line: Text HOME to 741741 International Association for Suicide Prevention: https://www.iasp.info/resources/Crisis_Centres/

Appendix B: Resources, Recommended Reading, and Glossary

PART 1: GLOSSARY OF KEY TERMS

Core Concepts Acknowledge

The first step of the Perspective Pivot. The practice of naming your thoughts, feelings, or physical sensations without judgment or trying to change them. Creates psychological distance from the spiral by labeling it as brain activity rather than objective truth. Activates the prefrontal cortex through the act of naming, which reduces amygdala activation.

Adjust

The second step of the Perspective Pivot. The practice of generating alternative perspectives by asking "What else could be true?" Creates cognitive flexibility by offering your brain multiple interpretations instead of accepting the first (usually catastrophic) one. Not about positive thinking—about creating options.

Align

The third step of the Perspective Pivot. The practice of taking one small action that moves you toward who you want to be, not away from what you fear. Restores sense of agency and interrupts rumination by shifting from thinking to doing. Action can be micro—standing up counts.

Amygdala

The brain's threat-detection center, often called the "smoke alarm." Activates the fight-flight-freeze response when it perceives danger (real or imagined). Can't distinguish between physical threats and psychological ones—treats public speaking and being chased by a predator as equivalent dangers. Goes offline through the Pivot's combination of naming, perspective-taking, and action.

Both/And Reframe

A cognitive flexibility technique used in the Adjust step of the Perspective Pivot. Rather than replacing a catastrophic thought with a positive one, the Both/And Reframe holds two possibilities simultaneously: "This might be true, and other things might also be true." Interrupts the brain's tendency toward certainty and binary thinking without requiring forced optimism. Rooted in dialectical thinking, which recognizes that two seemingly opposing things can coexist. Particularly effective when catastrophic thoughts feel too real to simply dismiss.

Catastrophic Thinking

A cognitive distortion where your brain automatically jumps to worst-case scenarios. Part of the brain's negativity bias—it's evolutionarily safer to assume the worst and be pleasantly surprised than to assume the best and be caught off guard. This is your brain trying to protect you, not a character flaw. The Pivot interrupts this pattern.

Cognitive Flexibility

The brain's ability to consider multiple perspectives and shift thinking patterns. Reduced when the amygdala is activated and increased when the prefrontal cortex is engaged. The Adjust step of the Pivot builds this capacity through repeated practice of generating alternative interpretations.

Crisis Pivot

Modified version of the Perspective Pivot for use during acute crisis when your nervous system is too dysregulated for the full framework. Uses simplified versions: Crisis Acknowledge (narrate facts), Crisis Adjust (identify 1% stabilizer), Crisis Align (smallest possible action). Not a lesser version—a necessary adaptation for high activation states.

Executive Function

A set of cognitive processes, including working memory, impulse control, task initiation, planning, organization, and emotional regulation. Managed primarily by the prefrontal cortex.Often impaired in ADHD, autism, and during high stress. The Pivot is designed to work even when executive function is compromised through physical anchors and simplified steps.

Imposter Syndrome

The persistent belief that you're not actually qualified or competent, that you've somehow fooled everyone, and that you'll eventually be "found out." Experienced by approximately 70% of high-achievers at some point. Not about lack of skill—it's a spiral pattern that discounts evidence of competence. Often hits hardest when you're succeeding.

Negativity Bias

The brain's tendency to prioritize negative information over positive information. Negative experiences are processed more deeply and remembered more vividly than positive ones. Ratio is approximately 5:1—you need five positive experiences to counterbalance one negative experience. Evolutionary adaptation that kept our ancestors alive, but makes modern humans prone to spiraling. The phrase: "Negativity always comes to the front of the line in our mind."

Neuroplasticity

The brain's ability to form new neural connections and reorganize existing ones throughout your lifetime. Means you can rewire thought patterns, but requires consistent practice (approximately 10,000 repetitions to fully automate a new behavior). Every time you use the Pivot, you're building new neural pathways and weakening old spiral pathways.

Perspective Pivot

The three-step framework (Acknowledge, Adjust, Align) for interrupting mental spirals and restoring cognitive clarity. Based on neuroscience research showing that naming emotions, generating alternatives, and taking action all reduce amygdala activation and increase prefrontal cortex engagement. Works in approximately three seconds once automated.

Polyvagal Theory

Dr. Stephen Porges' research on how the nervous system responds to safety and threat. Identifies three states: ventral vagal (social engagement/safety), sympathetic (fight-or-flight), and dorsal vagal (freeze/shutdown).

Understanding these states helps explain why cognitive tools don't work when your nervous system is in threat mode. The Pivot works by signaling safety to your nervous system through physical anchors, regulated breathing, and intentional action.

Prefrontal Cortex (PFC)

The brain's "executive center," responsible for rational thinking, decision-making, impulse control, and perspective-taking. Goes offline when the amygdala activates. The Perspective Pivot is designed to bring the PFC back online by interrupting the threat response through naming, perspective-generation, and values-based action.

Rejection Sensitive Dysphoria (RSD)

Extreme emotional sensitivity to perceived rejection, criticism, or failure. Common in ADHD and autism. Not about being "too sensitive"—it's a neurological difference in how the brain processes social threat. The emotional pain registers with the same intensity as physical pain.

Requires adapted Pivot strategies that acknowledge the neurological reality rather than dismissing the intensity.

Rumination

Repetitive, circular thinking about problems, mistakes, or worries without generating solutions. Keeps the amygdala activated and prevents the prefrontal cortex from problem-solving. Spiral thinking is a form of rumination. Distinguished from productive reflection by its circular, stuck quality and lack of forward movement.

Spiral (Mental Spiral)

A pattern of repetitive, escalating catastrophic thinking that pulls you away from the present moment and into worst-case scenarios. Characterized by "what if" thinking, black-and-white interpretations, and feeling stuck.

The Perspective Pivot interrupts spirals by creating cognitive space between trigger and response. Spirals aren't character flaws—they're learned neural pathways that can be rewired.

From Practice to Instinct

The state reached after months of consistent Pivot practice, where triggers lose their power to hijack you completely. Not the absence of spiraling, but the ability to catch spirals faster, recover quicker, and experience them with less intensity. Develops in three phases: Reactive Mastery, Preventive Awareness, and Embodied Resilience.

Measured in months and years, not weeks.

Triple-A Hand Hack

Physical gesture that represents the three steps of the Pivot. Thumbs and index fingers together forming a triangle (Acknowledge), thumbs break apart while index fingers stay touching (Adjust), index fingers point forward (Align). Provides a somatic anchor for the cognitive tool, remaining accessible even when the thinking brain is offline. Works through proprioception and muscle memory.

Window of Tolerance

Dr. Dan Siegel's concept describes the range of emotional activation where you can function optimally. Inside your window = able to think clearly and regulate emotions.

Outside your window = hyperarousal (panic, rage) or hypoarousal (shutdown, numbness). Crisis shrinks your window; Pivot practice expands it. Neurodivergent windows are often narrower, not because of deficiency but because of different neurological processing.

PART 2: RECOMMENDED READING

These books complement the Perspective Pivot by deepening your understanding of neuroscience, anxiety, behavior change, trauma, and resilience. You don't need to read everything—pick what addresses your specific needs.

ON NEUROSCIENCE AND THE BRAIN

Barrett,L. F. (2017). *How Emotions Are Made: The Secret Life of the Brain.* **Houghton Mifflin Harcourt.**

→ Revolutionizes understanding of emotions as constructed rather than hardwired. Essential for understanding why the Adjust step works—if emotions are predictions your brain makes, you can influence those predictions.

Eagleman,D. (2011). *Incognito: The Secret Lives of the Brain.* **Pantheon.**

→ Accessible neuroscience on how much of your brain's processing happens outside conscious awareness.

Explains why spirals feel automatic and why interrupting them requires deliberate practice.

Siegel, D. J. (2010). *Mindsight: The New Science of Personal Transformation.* **Bantam Books.**

→ Comprehensive guide to the window of tolerance and "name it to tame it" principle. Foundational for understanding emotional regulation and why Acknowledge works neurologically.

Porges, S. W. (2017). *The Pocket Guide to the Polyvagal Theory: The Transformative Power of Feeling Safe.* **W. W. Norton & Company.**

→ Accessible version of polyvagal theory. Explains why safety matters more than logic when you're spiraling.

Essential context for Chapter 5's nervous system healing section.

Sapolsky, R. M. (2004). *Why Zebras Don't Get Ulcers* (3rd ed.). **Henry Holt and Company.**

→ Definitive guide to stress biology. Explains why chronic stress (like constant spiraling) impacts physical health and why interrupting spirals matters for your body, not just your mind.

ON ANXIETY AND OVERTHINKING

Barlow, D. H., & Craske, M. G. (2007). *Mastery of Your Anxiety and Panic* **(4th ed.). Oxford University Press.**

→ Gold-standard workbook for panic and anxiety. Clinical but accessible. Excellent companion to the Pivot for understanding the physiology of anxiety.

Beck, J. S. (2011). *Cognitive Behavior Therapy: Basics and Beyond* **(2nd ed.). Guilford Press.**

→ The foundational CBT text. If you want to understand where cognitive reframing comes from and how the Pivot builds on CBT principles, start here.

Leahy, R. L. (2005). *The Worry Cure: Seven Steps to Stop Worry from Stopping You.* **Harmony Books.**

→ Specifically targets worry and rumination. Practical tools for chronic overthinkers. Complements the Pivot's approach to catastrophic thinking.

Wilson, K. G., & DuFrene, T. (2009). *Mindfulness for Two: An Acceptance and Commitment Therapy Approach to Mindfulness in Psychotherapy.* **New Harbinger Publications.**

→ ACT-based approach to thoughts. Complements the Pivot's Acknowledge step beautifully—thoughts as mental events rather than truth.

ON BEHAVIOR CHANGE AND HABIT FORMATION

Clear, J. (2018).*Atomic Habits: An Easy & Proven Way to Build Good Habits & Break Bad Ones.* **Avery.**

→ The definitive guide to habit formation. Use this to understand how to make the Pivot automatic (Chapter 8 principles). Particularly helpful for understanding cue-routine-reward loops.

Duhigg, C. (2012).*The Power of Habit: Why We Do What We Do in Life and Business.* **Random House.**

→ Explains the neuroscience of habit loops. Helpful for understanding why spiral patterns are so persistent and how to interrupt them at the cue level.

Prochaska, J. O., Norcross,J. C., & DiClemente, C. C. (1995). Changing for Good. William Morrow.

→ The stages of change model. Essential for understanding why relapse is normal (Chapter 8) and how change actually happens in stages, not overnight.

ON NEURODIVERGENCE (ADHD, AUTISM)

Barkley,R. A. (2015). *Taking Charge of Adult ADHD* (2nd ed.). Guilford Press.

→ Comprehensive, research-based guide to ADHD in adults. Not patronizing. Actually useful. Excellent context for understanding why standard Pivot instructions need adaptation for ADHD brains.

Hallowell,E. M., & Ratey, J. J. (2021).*ADHD 2.0: New Science and Essential Strategies for Thriving with Distraction.* **Ballantine Books.**

→ Updated research on ADHD with practical strategies. Good complement to Chapter 5. Particularly strong on ADHD and emotional regulation.

Price, D. (2022).*Unmasking Autism: Discovering the New Faces of Neuro-*

diversity. **Harmony Books.**

→ Particularly valuable for late-diagnosed autistic adults (many of whom discover diagnosis alongside ADHD).

Essential reading for understanding masking and its impact on nervous system regulation.

Solden, S. (2012). *Women with Attention Deficit Disorder*

(2nd ed.). Underwood Books.

→ Addresses how ADHD presents differently in women and why it's often missed until adulthood. Important context for spiral patterns rooted in years of misdiagnosed ADHD.

ON WORKPLACE PERFORMANCE AND BURNOUT

Brown, B. (2018).*Dare to Lead: BraveWork. Tough Conversations. Whole Hearts.* **Random House.**

→ Vulnerability and psychological safety in organizations. Essential context for Chapter 7's workplace spirals and how perfectionism develops in professional settings.

Cuddy, A. (2015). *Presence: Bringing Your Boldest Self to Your Biggest Challenges.* **Little, Brown and Company.**

→ Research on impostor syndrome and performance anxiety. Chapter 7 material. Particularly good on the mind-body connection in high-stakes situations.

Maslach, C., & Leiter, M. P. (2016). *The Burnout Challenge: Managing People's Relationships with Their Jobs.* **Harvard University Press.**

→ The researchers who defined burnout explain what it actually is and how to address it. Important distinction between burnout and spiraling (they're related but different).

Nagoski,E., & Nagoski,A. (2019). *Burnout: The Secret to Unlocking the Stress Cycle.* **Ballantine Books.**

→ Particularly good on the physiology of stress and why "just relax" doesn't work. Complements Chapter 5's nervous system regulation section beautifully.

ON TRAUMA AND NERVOUS SYSTEM REGULATION

Levine, P. A. (2010). *In an Unspoken Voice: How the Body Releases Trauma and Restores Goodness.* **North Atlantic Books.**

→ Somatic Experiencing approach. Explains why body-based regulation matters and why talking alone doesn't heal trauma. Essential for understanding Chapter 5's emphasis on somatic practices.

van der Kolk, B. (2014). *The Body Keeps the Score: Brain, Mind, and Body in the Healing of Trauma.* **Viking.**

→ The definitive trauma text. Essential for understanding why some spirals have roots in past experiences and require more than cognitive tools. The Pivot manages symptoms; trauma therapy addresses roots.

Dana, D. (2018). *The Polyvagal Theory in Therapy: Engaging the Rhythm of Regulation.* **W.W. Norton & Company.**

→ Clinical application of polyvagal theory. Especially relevant for crisis work (Chapter 6) and understanding when the Crisis Pivot is needed vs. the regular Pivot.

ON SELF-COMPASSION AND GROWTH

Neff, K. (2011). *Self-Compassion: The Proven Power of Being Kind to Yourself.* **William Morrow.**

→ Research-based guide to self-compassion. Antidoteto the harsh inner critic that fuels spirals. Particularly important for people who beat themselves up for spiraling.

Dweck, C. S. (2006). *Mindset: The New Psychology of Success.* **Random House.**

→ Growth mindset research. Helpful framing for Stage-4 progression (Chapter 8) and understanding that spiral patterns can be changed through practice.

Seligman, M. E. P. (2011). *Flourish: A Visionary New Understanding of Happiness and Well-being.* **FreePress.**

→ Positive psychology foundations. Context for why interrupting spirals matters for wellbeing and how the Pivot fits into a larger framework of human flourishing.

PART 4: PROFESSIONAL SUPPORT RESOURCES

Finding A Therapist

- Psychology Today TherapistFinder

https://www.psychologytoday.com/us/therapist s Search by location, insurance, specialty, and therapeutic approach. Most comprehensive database.

- SAMHSA Treatment Locator https://findtreatment.gov Government database of mental health and substance abuse treatment facilities.
- Open Path Collective https://openpathcollective.org Reduced-fee therapy ($30-$80 per session)for people without insurance.
- Inclusive Therapists

https://www.inclusivetherapists.com Directory specifically for BIPOC, LGBTQ+, and other marginalized communities.

- AANE (Asperger/Autism Network) https://www.aane.org Resources for autistic adults, including therapist referrals who understand neurodivergence.

- CHADD (Children and Adults with ADHD) <u>https://chadd.org/for-adul ts/</u> Professional directory and support resources for adults with ADHD.

Therapeutic Modalities That Complement The Pivot

- **Cognitive Behavioral Therapy (CBT)** Evidence-based approach that addresses thought patterns and behaviors. The Perspective Pivot is heavily influenced by CBT principles but designed for real-time use outside of therapy sessions.

- **Acceptance and Commitment Therapy (ACT)** Focuses on accepting what you can't control and committing to values-based action. The Acknowledge step aligns with ACT's "defusion" techniques. The Align step mirrors ACT's values-based action.

- **Dialectical Behavior Therapy (DBT)** Especially helpful for emotional regulation and distress tolerance. Good complement if you struggle with intense emotions or crisis situations (Chapter 6). The Crisis Pivot draws on DBT's crisis survival strategies.

- **Eye Movement Desensitization and Reprocessing (EMDR)** Trauma-specific therapy. Essential if your spirals are rooted in past traumatic experiences. The Pivot manages symptoms; EMDR addresses root causes.

- **Internal Family Systems (IFS)** Parts work therapy. Helpful if you notice different "voices" in your spiral (inner critic, scared child, perfectionist, etc.). Complements the Pivot's Acknowledge step by helping you identify which part is activated.

- **Somatic Experiencing (SE)** Body-based trauma therapy. Critical if your spirals have strong physical components or if you tend to freeze/shut down. Works beautifully with Chapter 5's nervous system regulation focus.

CRISIS RESOURCES (24/7 SUPPORT)

- 988 Suicide &Crisis Lifeline (US) Call or text: 988 https://988lifeline.org Free,confidential support for people in distress
- Crisis Text Line Text HOME to 741741 (US,Canada, UK) https://www.crisistextline.org 24/7 text-based crisis support
- SAMHSA National Helpline 1-800-662-4357 https://www.samhsa.gov/find-help/national-helpline Substance abuse and mental health referral service (English/Spanish)
- The Trevor Project (LGBTQ+ Youth) 1-866-488-7386 or text START to 678-678 https://www.thetrevorproject.org Crisis intervention and suicide prevention for LGBTQ+ young people
- National Domestic Violence Hotline 1-800-799-7233 or text START to 88788 https://www.thehotline.org If your spirals are related to relationship abuse
- Veterans Crisis Line Call 988 then press 1, or text 838255 https://www.veteranscrisisline.net Support for veterans and service members
- International Association for Suicide Prevention https://www.iasp.info/resources/Crisis_Centres/ Crisis centers by country (international resources)

Appendix C: The 30-Day Perspective Pivot Challenge

HOW TO USE THIS CHALLENGE

This 30-day program takes you from beginner to practitioner through progressive daily practice. This isn't about perfection; it's about building the neural pathway through consistent repetition.

What you'll need:

- 5-10 minutes per day
- A journal or note-taking app
- Willingness to practice even when you're not actively spiraling
- Permission to be imperfect (missing a day doesn't mean starting over)

The structure:

- Week 1: Building Awareness (Acknowledge) + Nervous System Foundation
- Week 2: Creating Flexibility (Adjust)
- Week 3: Taking Action (Align)
- Week 4: Integration and Real-World Application

Important notes:

- Practice each day's exercise, whether you're spiraling or not
- If you ARE spiraling on a given day, apply that day's focus to your actual spiral
- Missing days is normal; just pick up where you left off
- Track your progress using daily check boxes

NEURODIVERGENT ADAPTATIONS

Apply these modifications throughout the challenge as needed:

ADHD adaptations:

- Use voice memos instead of writing when your brain can't hold thoughts long enough
- Set alarms for practice times (time blindness makes remembering difficult)
- External reminders work better than internal (sticky notes, phone alerts, visual cues)
- Movement helps regulation; walk, pace, or move while practicing
- Write things down; don't rely on working memory
- Use physical objects(sticky notes, index cards) to externalize thinking
- Start with small increments if "one year from now" feels impossible

Autism adaptations:

- Create templates and use the same structure every time (reduces cognitive load)
- Write instead of speaking if that's easier
- Use categories and sort information into them (plays to your pattern recognition strength)
- For alexithymia: describe body sensations instead of emotion labels

- Practice hand gestures at home first before using them in public
- Set clear boundaries and time limits for predictability
- If generating multiple alternatives is difficult, 2-3 quality options is success

General neurodivergent support:

- Sensory regulation BEFORE cognitive Pivot (if you're at 8+ activation, regulate first)
- Honor truly microactions when executive function is compromised
- Build your personal micro-action library in advance
- Time limits reduce overwhelm (5-minute commitments, not marathon sessions)
- If "do the opposite" feels like a demand (PDA), reframe as curiosity: "What would happen if…?"

WEEK 1: BUILDINGAWARENESS + NERVOUS SYSTEM FOUNDATION

Goal: Notice spiral patterns without trying to change them. Build foundation skill of recognition. Establish nervous system regulation as the base for all Pivot work.

DAY 1: Spiral Inventory Set a timer for 5 minutes. Write down (stream-of-consciousness) every catastrophic thought pattern you remember having this past week.

Don't judge or solve them; just list them. Look for patterns: Are most about work, relationships, health, identity, or future uncertainty?

DAY 2: Nervous System Baseline Check Three times today (morning, midday, evening), pause and rate your nervous system activation on a 1-10 scale. Notice where you hold tension, how you're breathing, and your energy level. What's your average baseline? If you're consistently at 7+ before any trigger happens, you need nervous system regulation BEFORE cognitive techniques will work.

DAY 3: Naming Without Judging. Every time you catch yourself thinking something negative today, mentally reframe it. Instead of "I'm terrible at this," say "I'm having the thought that I'm terrible at this." Do this at least 5 times. This isn't about positive thinking; it's about accuracy. Thoughts are brain activity, not objective reality.

DAY 4: Body Scan for Spirals Set 3 alarms throughout the day. When each goes off, scan your body: chest, stomach, shoulders, jaw, breath. Write down what you notice. What are YOUR spiral signals? Do you always feel it in the same place?

DAY 5: The Spiral Trigger Log Every time you notice yourself spiraling today (or almost spiraling), write down: What happened right before? What time was it?

What was your first thought? What was your nervous system baseline before the trigger? Log at least 3 triggers with context.

DAY 6: Acknowledge Out Loud + Physical Anchor Next time you catch yourself spiraling: Form the triangle with your hands (thumbs and index fingers touching). Say out loud: "I am spiraling about [specific thing]. My body feels [physical sensation]. This is [anxiety/fear/overwhelm], not reality." If you can't speak out loud, write it while holding the hand gesture.

DAY 7: Week 1 Review + Nervous System Practice Review your notes from Days 1-6. Answer: What are my top 3 spiral patterns? Most common triggers?

What does spiraling feel like in my body? How quickly can I recognize when I'm spiraling? What's my average nervous system baseline? Then choose ONE nervous system regulation practice to do daily: bilateral movement, humming, weighted pressure, cold water, or gentle stretching.

WEEK 2: CREATING FLEXIBILITY (Learning to Adjust)

Goal: Generate alternative perspectives. Build cognitive flexibility—the ability to see multiple interpretations instead of accepting the first (catastrophic) one.

DAY 8: The "What Else Could Be True?" Question Pick one spiral from yesterday or today. Write down your catastrophic thought,then generate at least 3 alternatives. Example: "My boss didn't respond to my email. She's mad at me" becomes "She's busy / She doesn't need to respond / She's dealing with her own crisis and forgot." You don't have to believe the alternatives yet; just generate them.

DAY 9: The Best Friend Test When you catch yourself spiraling, imagine your best friend is telling you they're having this exact thought. What would you say to them? Write down what you're telling yourself versus what you'd tell your best friend. Do this at least twice. The compassion you extend to others? You deserve that too.

DAY 10: Evidence Collection Pick one recurring spiral. Write down your catastrophic thought, then list evidence FOR this thought and evidence AGAINST it. Be honest. Is there more evidence for or against? Anxiety feels like evidence, but it's not. Facts are evidence.

DAY 11: The 1-Year Test Next time you spiral, ask: "Will this matter in one year?" Write down what you're spiraling about and whether it will matter long-term. If no, why does it feel so urgent right now? This isn't about dismissing real problems; it's about right-sizing anxiety.

DAY 12: The "And" Practice Instead of "either/or" thinking, practice "both/and." Instead of "I messed up, therefore I'm incompetent," try "I messed up, AND I'm still competent." Practice this at least 3 times. Black-and-white thinking fuels spirals. "And" creates space for nuance.

DAY 13: Perspective Multiplication Pick one current spiral. Force yourself to generate 5 different perspectives. The first 2-3 are usually easy. The 4th and 5th require creativity and break your brain out of rigid patterns. Even if they feel unlikely, you're building the neural pathway for cognitive flexibility.

DAY 14: Week 2 Review + Nervous System Check-In Review your Week 2 notes. Which Adjust technique worked best? Which was hardest? Am I generating alternatives faster than a week ago? Have you been doing your daily regulation practice from Day 7?

Has your baseline activation level changed?

WEEK 3: TAKING ACTION (Learning to Align)

Goal: Move from thinking to doing. Build the muscle of taking small actions that restore your sense of agency.

DAY 15: The Smallest Possible Action Next time you spiral, ask: "What's the smallest possible thing I can do right now?" Examples: drink water, stand up, send one text, write one sentence, open the document, put on shoes. Do the action. Notice how it feels. Action doesn't have to be big to be effective.

DAY 16: The One-Thing Rule When you catch yourself spiraling about everything you need to do, ask: "If I could only do ONE thing right now, what would have the most impact?" Choose that one thing. Do it. Then reassess. Overwhelm spirals often come from trying to solve everything at once.

DAY 17: The 5-Minute Commitment Pick something you've been avoiding. Commit to 5 minutes. Set a timer. Do the thing for exactly 5 minutes. When the timer goes off, you can stop. Often, the hardest part is starting. Five minutes makes starting feel manageable.

DAY 18: Action as Experiment Choose one action you've been spiraling about. Reframe it as an experiment: "I'm going to try [action] and see what happens. I'm collecting data, not trying to be perfect." Do the action.

Write down what you learned. Experiments can't fail; they only generate information.

DAY 19: The Opposite Action Notice what your spiral is urging you to do (avoid, hide, stay in bed, cancel plans, isolate, overwork). Do the opposite. If your spiral says "hide," reach out to someone. If it says "overwork," take a break. Did the catastrophic prediction come true?

DAY 20: Body-First Action Next time you spiral, do something physical BEFORE trying to think your way out: walk for 5 minutes, do jumping jacks, shake out your limbs, dance to one song, do push-ups. Then try to Pivot. Was it easier after moving your body? You can't think your way out of a threat response.

DAY 21: Week 3 Review + Integration Check Review Week 3. Which Align technique was most effective? When did taking action feel hardest? Did action reduce spiraling, even when actions were tiny? Can I now use all three steps (Acknowledge-Adjust-Align) together?

WEEK 4: INTEGRATION AND REAL-WORLD APPLICATION

Goal: Apply the full framework in challenging real-world situations. Build toward automaticity.

DAY 22: Morning Ritual Integration Add the Pivot to your morning routine. Before checking your phone: Form the triangle. Acknowledge your current state ("I'm feeling [rested/anxious/groggy/calm/activated]"). Adjust one yesterday thought ("Yesterday I thought [X].

What else could be true: [Y]"). Align with today's intention ("Today I will [one specific action]"). Do this every morning this week.

DAY 23: The Work Pivot Use the Pivot on one work-related spiral today. Before a meeting, after a difficult email, when you notice imposter syndrome, or after making a mistake. Apply all three steps. Write down how it went. Can you use this tool at work without anyone noticing?

DAY 24: The Relationship Pivot Use the Pivot on one relationship spiral today. After a difficult conversation, when someone doesn't text back, when you feel rejected, or when you're replaying what you said.

Apply all three steps. Write down what happened.

DAY 25: The High-Pressure Pivot Today, intentionally use the Pivot in a high-pressure situation. During a presentation, in a difficult conversation, while making an important decision, or in a triggering social situation. This is the real test. Did it work when stakes were high?

DAY 26: The Crisis Pivot If you're in actual crisis today, use the simplified Crisis Pivot: Crisis Acknowledge (narrate facts only), Crisis Adjust ("What do I need right now to get 1% more stable?"), Crisis Align (do the smallest possible thing). If you're NOT in crisis, write down your Crisis Pivot plan for when you need it.

DAY 27: The Relapse Recovery Think about a recent time you spiraled for hours or days and completely forgot you had this tool. Use the Pivot to address the relapse itself. Acknowledge: "I forgot to use the Pivot. I'm frustrated with myself." Adjust: "Relapse is normal. Old patterns are strong. This doesn't erase my progress." Align: "Right now, I'm going to use the Pivot on whatever I'm currently spiraling about."

DAY 28: Teaching the Pivot Explain the framework to one person: Acknowledge, Adjust, Align. Show them the Triple-A Hand Hack. Share why it's helping you. Walk them through an example. Teaching is the ultimate test of understanding.

DAY 29: From Practice to Instinct Reflect on how your spiraling has changed over the past month. Do you catch spirals faster? Do they feel less intense? Do you recover more quickly? Are certain triggers losing their power? Can you use the Pivot in public/high-pressure situations? Do you sometimes Pivot automatically?

Immunity doesn't mean spirals stop; it means they don't hijack you completely.

DAY 30: Final Reflection and Integration Review your entire month. How have my spirals changed (frequency, intensity, duration)? Which Pivot step is easiest now? Which still requires conscious effort? What's my biggest win? What surprised me? Where do I still struggle? What's my plan for continuing this practice?

Create your ongoing practice plan: daily morning/evening practice, highest-risk spiral days, crisis protocol, accountability partner, non-negotiable neurodivergent adaptations.

POST-CHALLENGE: WHAT'S NEXT?

Continue options:

- Repeat the challenge with bigger, more complex spirals
- Use Morning Practice and Evening Review from Appendix A daily
- Focus on your weakest step (Acknowledge, Adjust, or Align) for a dedicated week
- Teach the Pivot to friends, family, or colleagues
- If spirals are rooted in trauma, consider therapy alongside the Pivot

Signs the Pivot is integrating:

- You catch spirals within minutes instead of hours
- You use the framework without consciously thinking "Acknowledge, Adjust, Align"

- Other people notice you seem less reactive
- You recover from spirals faster
- You can function during spirals instead of being completely derailed
- You practice on small spirals automatically
- Your nervous system baseline has lowered

If you're struggling:

- Review the troubleshooting guide in Appendix A
- Consider whether you need neurodivergent adaptations (see Chapter 5)
- Assess whether your nervous system baseline is too high for cognitive tools to work
- Assess whether you need additional support (therapy, medication, crisis intervention)
- Remember: progress isn't linear; relapses are part of the process
- Check if you're skipping Acknowledge (most common mistake)

CELEBRATION

You did 30 days of deliberate cognitive practice. That matters.

Most people read about tools and never practice them. You practiced. Most people try something once and quit when it's hard. You kept going. Most people know what they should do, but don't build the habit. You built the habit.

The Perspective Pivot is now part of your cognitive toolkit.

You won't use it perfectly. You'll forget sometimes.

You'll relapse. That's all normal.

But you now have a framework for interrupting spirals, creating cognitive flexibility, and taking action when your brain wants you to stay stuck.

That's not small. That's revolutionary.

Keep going. Use the Pivot daily on big spirals and small ones. Keep practicing even when it feels like you "should" be past this by now.

Remember: Acknowledge creates space, Adjust creates options, Align creates momentum

Three steps. Three seconds.One choice at a time.

You're building spiral immunity. It takes 6+ months to fully integrate.

You've got this.

Where neuroscience meets soul, you're rewiring your brain one pivot at a time.

Appendix D: Case Studies—The Pivot In Action

HOW TO USE THIS APPENDIX

The following case studies show real applications of The Perspective Pivot across different situations, demographics, and spiral types. These are composite cases drawn from nearly two decades of client work, coaching sessions, and workshop participants. All identifying details have been changed to protect privacy.

You may see yourself in multiple case studies. Most people don't have just one spiral type. Pick the stories that resonate most and notice what tools worked for each person.

CASE STUDY 1: SARAH—THE WORKPLACE IMPOSTER

Background: Sarah, 34, is a senior project manager at a tech company. Promoted six months ago, she's been spiraling ever since despite an MBA from a top school and consistently strong performance reviews.

Primary spiral: "I don't actually know what I'm doing. Everyone else is more qualified. Eventually, they'll realize I shouldn't be in this role. Every mistake proves I don't belong here."

Physical symptoms: Racing heart before meetings, chest tightness when presenting, difficulty sleeping Sunday nights, and constant shoulder tension. Nervous system baseline: 7/10 most days, spiking to 9/10 before high-stakes meetings.

The Turning Point: Sarah's spiral peaked before a quarterly leadership presentation. Three minutes before presenting, she used the Triple-A Hand Hack in the bathroom:

- ACKNOWLEDGE (forming triangle): "I am spiraling about this presentation. My brain is catastrophizing. My heart is racing. This is anxiety, not prophecy."
- ADJUST (thumbs break apart): "What else could be true? I've done excellent prep. I've presented successfully dozens of times before. My nervousness doesn't mean I'm unprepared; it means I care. The last three presentations I stressed about went fine."
- ALIGN (index fingers forward): "I'm going to review my opening line one more time, then take three slow breaths. Then I'm walking in and doing my job."

The presentation went well. Not perfect—she stumbled over one slide—but she recovered. More importantly, she didn't spiral about the stumble afterward. For the first time, she had evidence that she could be nervous AND competent simultaneously.

Practice & Challenges For the first month, Sarah would forget to use the framework until after she'd already spiraled for hours.

What helped her progress:

- Morning practice during her commute on something small from the day before
- Pre-meeting protocol: 5-minute alarm before high-stakes meetings to Acknowledge anxiety, Adjust by reviewing evidence of competence, Align by identifying her one main message
- Evening spiral review: noting triggers revealed patterns (vague feedback from her boss, comparing herself to specific colleagues, late Sunday nights)
- Nervous system work: 10 minutes of bilateral walking every morning

dropped her baseline from 7/10 to 5/10 within six weeks

- Pivot partner: trusted colleague who would check in: "Are you spiraling or is this a real concern?"

Biggest struggle: Sarah kept skipping Acknowledge and jumping straight to Adjust. She'd try to talk herself out of anxiety without first naming it. Her therapist pointed out: "You can't change what you haven't acknowledged." The physical gesture of forming the triangle forced the pause.

Relapse moment: Four months in, after legitimately difficult feedback from her boss about a project delay, Sarah spiraled for three days about being fired and completely forgot about the Pivot. Her colleague asked: "Have you Pivoted on this or are you just spinning?" Sarah used it immediately, and the spiral broke within 20 minutes.

Current Status (10 months) Sarah still experiences imposter syndrome, but now catches it within minutes instead of spiraling for days. She can present to executives without catastrophizing, receive critical feedback without interpreting it as "I'm about to be fired," and her Sunday night anxiety dropped by 70%. Her nervous system baseline is now 4-5/10 instead of 7/10.

Her words: "I used to think the goal was to feel completely confident all the time. Now I realize confidence isn't the absence of doubt; it's knowing how to work with doubt when it shows up. I still have imposter thoughts. I just don't let them run my life anymore."

CASE STUDY 2: MARCUS—THE CRISIS NAVIGATOR

Background Marcus, 41, nonprofit director and single father of two teenagers. When his marriage ended unexpectedly after 16 years, Marcus experienced his first true mental health crisis.

Primary spiral: "My entire life is falling apart. I'm failing my kids. I'm going to lose my house. I can't do this alone. I'll never recover from this."

Physical symptoms: Sleeping only 2-3 hours at a time, lost 15 pounds in three weeks, panic attacks in his car, complete loss of appetite, feeling like he was "watching his life from outside his body." Nervous system baseline: 10/10 for weeks. Pure survival mode.

The Crisis Pivot Journey: Marcus didn't have one turning point where the Pivot solved everything. He had dozens of small moments where it kept him functional when he wanted to completely shut down.

Week 1 - Survival Mode: Marcus couldn't use the full Pivot—his nervous system was too dysregulated. His therapist taught him the Crisis Pivot:

- Crisis Acknowledge: "I'm sitting in my car outside my house. My chest is tight. I'm crying. It's Tuesday at 6 PM. My kids are inside. I'm safe in this moment even though nothing feels safe."
- Crisis Adjust: "What do I need in the next 60 seconds to get 1% more stable? I need to breathe. I need to drink this water. I need to text my brother and say, 'I'm not okay.'"
- Crisis Align: "I'm going to walk inside. That's it. Just walk inside."

He used this version 10-15 times daily for the first two weeks. Sometimes it was: "I'm going to get out of bed. I'm going to feed my kids breakfast. I'm going to show up to work even though I feel like I'm underwater."

Week 2-4 - Building Capacity: As his nervous system stabilized slightly (from 10/10 to 8/10), Marcus started using the regular Pivot on smaller spirals: "I'm spiraling about money. I'm terrified about the mortgage. But right now, today, I have enough. I'm going to review my budget with my financial advisor next week. Today I'm just going to get through today."

Months 2-6 - Recovery and Integration: Marcus built a daily practice. Morning: acknowledge his emotional state without judgment. Evening: identify what he was grateful survived that day (even if it was just "I fed my kids and got them to school").

Practice & Challenges

What helped Marcus:

- Crisis Pivot for acute moments when the full framework was inaccessible
- Therapy twice a week
- EMDR for divorce trauma (Pivot managed symptoms; EMDR addressed roots)
- Brother as accountability partner and crisis contact
- Medication for the first three months to stabilize sleep and panic
- Distinguishing between grief (which needed to be felt) and catastrophic spirals (which needed to be interrupted)

Biggest struggle: Marcus felt like he "should" be handling the crisis better. He spiraled about spiraling. His therapist reframed: "You're not supposed to handle your marriage ending 'well.' You're supposed to survive it.

And you are."

Current Status (18 months) Marcus still has hard days. Grief doesn't follow a timeline. But he's no longer in crisis mode. He rebuilt his life differently—simpler routines, clearer boundaries, more support. He co-parents effectively with his ex-wife. His kids are adjusting.

His words: "The Pivot didn't make my divorce hurt less. It gave me a way to function through the pain instead of being consumed by it. There's a difference between feeling the grief and spiraling about the grief. I learned to tell them apart."

CASE STUDY 3: AISHA—THE NEURODIVERGENT ADAPTER

Background: Aisha, 28, software engineer, diagnosed with ADHD at 26 and autism at 27. Describes her brain as "5,000 tabs open at once, all playing different music, and I can't close any of them."

Primary spiral: "Everyone thinks I'm lazy/weird/difficult. I'm trying so hard, and no one sees it. I can't do basic things everyone else does easily.

What's wrong with me?"

Physical symptoms: Sensory overwhelm (sounds, lights, textures), executive dysfunction, time blindness (4 hours feels like 20 minutes), meltdowns/shutdowns when overstimulated, extreme rejection sensitivity. Nervous system baseline: 8/10 most days due to chronic masking and sensory overload.

The Adapted Pivot: Aisha tried using the Perspective Pivot as written. It didn't work. Her ADHD brain wouldn't hold the steps internally; her executive dysfunction paralyzed the Align step. Her therapist said, "The tool isn't wrong. You're not wrong. You need the neurodivergent version."

- ACKNOWLEDGE (External): Aisha can't just think her acknowledgments. She has to externalize through voice memos on her phone, texting herself, writing with a marker on her bathroom mirror, or drawing the spiral as a picture. Externalizing moves thoughts from "brain soup" to concrete data she can see/hear.
- ADJUST (Visual/Physical): Aisha writes the catastrophic thought on a sticky note, then writes 3-4 alternative perspectives on separate sticky notes and physically moves them around spatially. The kinesthetic processing helps her ADHD brain track multiple perspectives. The systematic approach works for her autistic brain.
- ALIGN (Micro-Steps + Body Doubling): Aisha breaks actions into absurdly small steps ("Click inbox icon" → "Find email" → "Click reply" → "Type 'Hi'"), uses 5-minute timers, body doubles on video calls with friends working silently, and links new actions to existing routines. ADHD brains need external structure and accountability.

Practice & Challenges For two months, Aisha felt ridiculous using all these adaptations. Her breakthrough came when her therapist reframed: "Neurotypical people have accommodations too; theirs are just baked into the environment because society is designed for their brains."

What helped her progress:

- ADHD-specific Pivot journal template in Notes app
- Sensory-first regulation (weighted blanket,noise-canceling headphones, dim lights) before attempting cognitive tools
- RSD protocol: tracking "RSD False Alarms" to build evidence against catastrophic interpretations
- Time-based modifications: hourly alarms asking "Am I spiraling right now?" because time blindness made tracking impossible
- Unmasking practice: using accommodations at work so she had capacity for evening spirals

Biggest struggle: Perfectionism about using the tool "right." Aisha beat herself up for "needing so many modifications." She had to learn: there is no "right" way, only what works for your brain.

Autistic advantage: Her pattern recognition skills excelled at spiral tracking. After two months, she identified her top triggers: unclear instructions at work, ambiguous social cues, being late, sensory overwhelm, and rejection. Knowing patterns helped her catch spirals earlier.

Current Status (10 months) Aisha still spirals regularly—her ADHD and autism mean her nervous system is more reactive. But she recovers faster and doesn't spiral about spiraling. She handles ambiguous feedback at work without assuming she's getting fired, advocates for what she needs (clear instructions, written communication, flexible deadlines), and stopped comparing herself to neurotypical productivity standards. Her nervous system baseline dropped from 8/10 to 5-6/10.

Her words: "I used to think the goal was to not need tools. Now I realize neurotypical people have tools too; theirs are just baked into the environment. My tools aren't evidence that I'm broken. They're evidence I'm learning how to work with my actual brain, not the brain I wish I had."

CASE STUDY 4: DR. KENJI—THE PERFECTIONIST PHYSICIAN

Background Dr. Kenji, 39, emergency medicine physician. Excellent at his job, calm under pressure, decisive in critical moments—at work.At home, he falls apart.

Primary spiral: "I made a mistake. What if I missed something? What if that patient has a complication? What if I'm not as good as I think I am? One mistake and someone could die."

Physical symptoms: Can't turn off his brain after shifts, replays cases obsessively, wakes up at 3 AM, catastrophizing about medical errors, stress headaches, and high blood pressure. Nervous system baseline: 7-8/10 due to high-stakes work environment.

The Turning Point Kenji experienced a near-miss—he almost prescribed a medication that would have caused an allergic reaction, but caught it at the last second. No harm occurred. But he spiraled for two weeks.

His therapist introduced the Pivot and addressed his perfectionism: "You're holding yourself to a standard that doesn't exist. Zero mistakes is not human. Zero mistakes is not medicine. The goal isn't perfection; it's best practice given imperfect information."

His first Pivot:

- ACKNOWLEDGE: "I'm ruminating about this near-miss. I'm terrified I'm going to make a fatal error. I feel like I can't trust myself. My body has been tight for two weeks."
- ADJUST: "What else could be true? I CAUGHT the error—that's the system working. I've successfully treated thousands of patients. One near-miss doesn't negate competence. Medicine is practiced under uncertainty by imperfect humans. Would I judge a colleague this harshly for catching their own error?"
- ALIGN: "I'm going to document this near-miss in my learning log, review my allergy-check protocol with my team to strengthen the system, then close this loop today."

Practice & Challenges Kenji's perfectionism made the Pivot difficult—he wanted to do the Pivot perfectly.

What helped him progress:

- *Post-shift protocol:* driving home in silence, doing mental Pivot on any cases he was ruminating about. By the time he walked in the door, he'd processed the day. This created a boundary: "Work stays in the car."
- "Perfect is not the goal" mantra: repeatedly reminding himself the Pivot doesn't need to be done perfectly
- *Peer consultation group:* hearing other excellent physicians share their mistakes normalized imperfection
- *Nervous system regulation:* Brazilian jiu-jitsu twice weekly (physical discharge + present-moment focus), no phone for the first hour after getting home, therapy every other week. Baseline dropped from 7-8/10 to 5-6/10.

Biggest struggle: Kenji's professional identity was wrapped up in being "the doctor who doesn't make mistakes." Using the Pivot meant accepting he's human, which felt like admitting weakness.

His mentor reframed: "The best doctors aren't the ones who never make mistakes. They're the ones who catch mistakes, learn from them, and don't let fear paralyze them. Your rumination isn't keeping patients safe. It's keeping you anxious."

After a particularly brutal stretch (multiple patient deaths in one week, including a child), Kenji couldn't Pivot—he was numb, not spiraling.

He learned: the Pivot works for spiraling, but compassion fatigue/burnout requires different interventions (therapy, time off, peer support, boundaries).

Current Status (11 months) Kenji still has hard shifts, but he doesn't carry every case home anymore. He can leave work at work (most days), stopped waking up at 3 AM replaying cases, and can acknowledge uncertainty without catastrophizing. His blood pressure dropped, his marriage improved, and he remembered why he went into medicine. His nervous system baseline is 4-5/10 instead of 7-8/10.

His words: "I used to think the Pivot was about positive thinking—just convince yourself everything is fine. It's not. It's about distinguishing between useful concern (Did I follow best practice?) and useless catastrophizing (I'm a terrible doctor). The first makes me better. The second just makes me anxious and worse at my job."

Appendix E: Reflection Questions

HOW TO USE THIS SECTION

This appendix contains reflection questions for every chapter in The Perspective Pivot. You can use these questions in three ways:

- **Personal Reflection:** Work through questions as you read, using them as journaling prompts to deepen your understanding and track your growth.
- **Book Club Discussion:** Use these as conversation starters for group discussion. Each chapter includes questions designed to spark meaningful dialogue about shared experiences and different perspectives.
- **Periodic Review:** Return to these questions weeks or months into your practice. Your answers will evolve as your relationship with spiraling changes.

Each chapter includes three types of questions:

- **Behavioral:** Action-focused questions about what you do and what you might change
- **Emotional:** Feeling-focused questions about your internal experience
- **Reflective:** Insight-focused questions that invite deeper self-awareness

You don't have to answer every question. Choose the ones that resonate. Skip the ones that don't. This is your practice.

INTRODUCTION: THE THREE-SECOND REVOLUTION

- **Behavioral:** What's one specific situation in the past week where claiming a three-second window could have changed your response?
- **Emotional:** How does it feel to read that your spiral voice isn't evidence of weakness but predictable biology?
- **Reflective:** If you could reclaim just one pattern of catastrophic thinking, which would have the biggest impact on your daily life?

PART I: THE PROBLEM

CHAPTER 1: THE SPIRAL TRAP

- **Behavioral:** What's one spiral pattern you recognized in yourself while reading this chapter?
- **Emotional:** How does it feel to know your spiraling is neurology, not a character flaw?
- **Reflective:** Wherein your life does negativity most often "come to the front of the line"?

PART II: THE SOLUTION

CHAPTER 2: THE THREE-SECOND SOLUTION

- **Behavioral:** When you practiced the Triple-A Hand Hack for the first time, what did you notice in your body?
- **Emotional:** What resistance came up when you tried the physical gestures? Did they feel awkward, silly, or surprisingly grounding?
- **Reflective:** Which of the three steps (Acknowledge, Adjust, Align) feels most natural to you right now, and which feels most challenging?

CHAPTER 3: ADJUST AND ALIGN

- **Behavioral:** Choose one catastrophic thought you had this week. Walk it through the Evidence Lawyer technique. What did you discover?
- **Emotional:** How does it feel to hold two truths at once (the "both/and" practice) instead of forcing either/or thinking?
- **Reflective:** When you think about your spiral voice, what is it trying to protect you from? What old wound might be driving your brain's threat detection?

PART III: MAKING IT LAST

CHAPTER 4: MAKING IT AUTOMATIC

- **Behavioral:** What's one small, daily trigger where you can practice the Pivot this week?
- **Emotional:** How do you feel about the timeline, that this might take six months or more to become automatic?
- **Reflective:** Which stage are you in right now: Unconscious Incompetence, Conscious Incompetence, Conscious Competence, or Unconscious Competence?

CHAPTER 5: THE NEURODIVERGENT PIVOT

- **Behavioral:** What's one adaptation from this chapter you'll implement immediately?
- **Emotional:** How does it feel to have tools designed for your brain, not forced to fit it?
- **Reflective:** What would change if you stopped trying to regulate like a neurotypical person and started working with your actual neurology?

CHAPTER 6: WHEN LIFE HITS HARD

- **Behavioral:** What's your Crisis Pivot plan for the next genuinely hard thing that happens?
- **Emotional:** Where are you conflating pain (inevitable)with suffering (optional) right now?
- **Reflective:** What grief are you carrying that you've been calling anxiety?

CHAPTER 7: THE PIVOT AT WORK

- **Behavioral:** What's your highest-risk workplace spiral trigger, and what would a pre-emptive Pivot look like for that situation?
- **Emotional:** How much of your self-worth is currently tied to your professional performance? Does that percentage feel healthy or unsustainable?
- **Reflective:** If you could separate your job performance from your human worth completely, how would your relationship with work stress change?

CHAPTER 8: FROM PRACTICE TO INSTINCT

- **Behavioral:** What evidence do you have that spiral immunity is beginning to develop, even in small ways?
- **Emotional:** How does it feel to know that mastery looks like skilled navigation, not perfect avoidance?
- **Reflective:** What identity shift is happening as you practice the Pivot? Who are you becoming through this work?

FOR BOOK CLUBS: CONVERSATION STARTERS

These open-ended questions work well for group discussion and can be used regardless of which chapter you're discussing.

Opening Questions (Use at the beginning of any session):

- What's one thing that surprised you in this section?
- Did anything in these chapters challenge something you previously believed about anxiety, spiraling, or your own brain?
- What's one concept you're still wrestling with or want to understand better?

Connection Questions (Help people share experiences):

- Who else has experienced [specific spiral pattern discussed]? What does it feel like for you?
- How do different people in this group experience the same trigger differently?
- What adaptations or modifications have you made to the Pivot to fit your life or brain?

Application Questions (Move from theory to practice):

- What's one way you've used the Pivots since our last meeting? How did it go?
- Where did you struggle this week? What got in the way of using the tool?
- What would support or accountability look like for you as you practice this?

Depth Questions (For groups ready to go deeper):

- How has your relationship with your own mind shifted since starting this book?
- What old stories about yourself are you beginning to question?
- Where do you see the connection between personal healing and collective contribution in this work?

Closing Questions (Use at the end of any session):

- What's one thing you're taking away from today's discussion?
- What's one practice or commitment you're making for the week ahead?
- How can this group support you?

FOR JOURNALING: 30-DAY REFLECTION

PROMPTS

Use these prompts alongside the 30-Day Perspective Pivot Challenge in Appendix C, or work through them at your own pace.

WEEK 1: AWARENESS

- Day 1: Write about a recent spiral in detail. What triggered it? How did it feel in your body? How long did it last?
- Day 2: What's your earliest memory of catastrophic thinking? How far back does this pattern go?
- Day 3: If your spiral voice had a name and personality, what would it be? Describe it like a character.
- Day 4: What does your spiral voice sound like? Whose voice from your past does it resemble?
- Day 5: What are you most afraid will happen if you stop catastrophizing?
- Day 6: Where in your body do you feel spirals most intensely? Draw or describe the physical sensation.
- Day 7: What pattern did you notice this week that you hadn't seen before?

WEEK 2: UNDERSTANDING

- Day 8: What purpose has catastrophic thinking served in your life? How has it tried to protect you?
- Day 9: Write a letter from your spiral voice explaining why it does what

it does.

- Day 10: What would it mean about you if spiraling really is just neurology, not character failure?
- Day 11: How did your childhood shape your current spiral patterns?
- Day 12: What environments or people tend to lower your spiral threshold? What raises it?
- Day 13: If you could tell your younger self one thing about spiraling, what would it be?
- Day 14: What shifted for you this week?

WEEK 3: PRACTICING

- Day 15: Describe one successful Pivot in detail. What made it work?
- Day 16: Describe one time you forgot to use the Pivot and spiraled anyway. What happened? What did you learn?
- Day 17: Which step is easiest for you: Acknowledge, Adjust, or Align? Why?
- Day 18: Which step is hardest? What makes it challenging?
- Day 19: How is your spiral voice responding to you learning this tool? Is it resisting?
- Day 20: What would complete spiral immunity look like for you?
- Day 21: What evidence do you have that you're changing, even in small ways?

WEEK 4: INTEGRATING

- Day 22: How has your relationship with uncertainty shifted since you started practicing?
- Day 23: What triggers used to send you into three-day spirals that now barely register?
- Day 24: Write about a moment when you caught a spiral at the trigger point, before it fully formed.
- Day 25: How has learning the Pivot changed your relationships?

- Day 26: What are you becoming as you practice this work?
- Day 27: If you could go back to the beginning of this book, what would you tell yourself?
- Day 28: What do you know now about your brain that you didn't know 30 days ago?
- Day 29: What does freedom from spiraling look like for you? Not perfection, but skilled navigation.
- Day 30: Write a letter to yourself six months from now. What do you hope will be different? What do you want to remember?

BONUS: QUESTIONS FOR SPECIFIC SITUATIONS

For Relationship Spirals:

- What story am I telling myself about this person's behavior?
- What past relationship wound might be activated right now?
- Am I responding to what's actually happening or to what I'm afraid might happen?

For Workplace Spirals:

- Is this based on actual feedback or my own fear?
- Would I judge a colleague this harshly for the same thing?
- What's the smallest professional action I can take right now that restores my sense of capability?

For Identity Spirals:

- What am I making this moment mean about my entire worth?
- If I removed achievement/productivity/performance from the equation, who am I?
- What would unconditional self-worth feel like?

For Crisis Moments:

- What's actually happening right now, in this moment?
- What do I need in the next 60 seconds to get one percent more stable?
- Who are my safe people, and have I reached out?

FINAL REFLECTION

After finishing the book and working with these questions, consider:

- How has your understanding of your own mind changed?
- What's different about your relationship with catastrophic thinking?
- What practices are you committed to continuing?
- What support do you need to maintain this work?
- How will you know if you're building spiral immunity?

Remember: This work isn't about perfection. It's about building the skill to navigate spirals when they come, recovering faster when you fall, and trusting that you're more capable than your anxious mind will ever admit.

The revolution continues, one three-second window at a time.

References

Arnsten, A. F. T. (2009). Stress signalling pathways that impair prefrontal cortex structure and function. *Nature Reviews Neuroscience, 10*(6), 410–422. https://doi.org/10.1038/nrn2648

Arnsten, A. F. T., Raskind, M. A., Taylor, F. B., & Connor, D. F. (2015). The effects of stress exposure on prefrontal cortex: Translating basic research into successful treatments for post-traumatic stress disorder. *Neurobiology of Stress, 1*, 89–99. https://doi.org/10.1016/j.ynstr.2014.10.002

Bandura, A. (1977). Self-efficacy: Toward a unifying theory of behavioral change. *Psychological Review, 84*(2), 191–215. https://doi.org/10.1037/0033-295X.84.2.191

Barlow, D. H. (2002). *Anxiety and its disorders: The nature and treatment of anxiety and panic* (2nd ed.). Guilford Press.

Barkley, R. A. (2015). *Attention-deficit hyperactivity disorder: A handbook for diagnosis and treatment* (4th ed.). Guilford Press.

Barrett, L. F. (2017). *How emotions are made: The secret life of the brain.* Houghton Mifflin Harcourt.

Baumeister, R. F., Bratslavsky, E., Finkenauer, C., & Vohs, K. D. (2001). Bad is stronger than good. *Review of General Psychology, 5*(4), 323–370. https://doi.org/10.1037/1089-2680.5.4.323

Beck, A. T. (1976). *Cognitive therapy and the emotional disorders.* International Universities Press.

Brown, T. E. (2013). *A new understanding of ADHD in children and adults: Executive function impairments.* Routledge.

Burns, D. D. (1980). *Feeling good: The new mood therapy.* William Morrow.

Cassidy, S., Bradley, L., Shaw, R., & Baron-Cohen, S. (2018). Risk markers for suicidality in autistic adults. *Molecular Autism, 9*(1), Article 42. https://doi.org/10.1186/s13229-018-0226-4

Clark, A. (2013). Whatever next? Predictive brains, situated agents, and the future of cognitive science. *Behavioral and Brain Sciences, 36*(3), 181–204. https://doi.org/10.1017/S0140525X12000477

Craig, A. D. (2009). How do you feel — now? The anterior insula and human awareness. *Nature Reviews Neuroscience, 10*(1), 59–70. https://doi.org/10.1038/nrn2555

Damasio, A. R. (1994). *Descartes' error: Emotion, reason, and the human brain.* G. P. Putnam's Sons.

Dodson, W. (2022). How ADHD ignites rejection sensitive dysphoria. *ADDitude Magazine.* https://www.additudemag.com/rejection-sensitive-dysphoria-adhd-emotional-dysregulation/

Dweck, C. S. (2006). *Mindset: The new psychology of success.* Random House.

Fredrickson, B. L. (2001). The role of positive emotions in positive psychology: The broaden-and-build theory of positive emotions. *American Psychologist, 56*(3), 218–226. https://doi.org/10.1037/0003-066X.56.3.218

Gilbert, D. T., & Wilson, T. D. (2007). Prospection: Experiencing the future. *Science, 317*(5843), 1351–1354. https://doi.org/10.1126/science.1144161

Goldin-Meadow, S., & Alibali, M. W. (2013). Gesture's role in speaking, learning, and creating language. *Annual Review of Psychology, 64,* 257–283. https://doi.org/10.1146/annurev-psych-113011-143802

Grandin, T. (2006). *Thinking in pictures: My life with autism* (Expanded ed.). Vintage Books.

Hanson, R. (2013). *Hardwiring happiness: The new brain science of contentment, calm, and confidence.* Harmony Books.

Hayes, S. C., Strosahl, K. D., & Wilson, K. G. (2011). *Acceptance and commitment therapy: The process and practice of mindful change* (2nd ed.). Guilford Press.

Hebb, D. O. (1949). *The organization of behavior: A neuropsychological theory.* Wiley.

Hudson, C. C., Hall, L., & Harkness, K. L. (2019). Prevalence of depressive disorders in individuals with autism spectrum disorder: A meta-analysis. *Journal of Abnormal Child Psychology, 47*(1), 165–175. https://doi.org/10.1007/s10802-018-0402-1

Kabat-Zinn, J. (1990). *Full catastrophe living: Using the wisdom of your body and mind to face stress, pain, and illness.* Delta.

Kessler, D. (2019). *Finding meaning: The sixth stage of grief.* Scribner.

Lally, P., van Jaarsveld, C. H. M., Potts, H. W. W., & Wardle, J. (2010). How are habits formed: Modelling habit formation in the real world. *European Journal of Social Psychology, 40*(6), 998–1009. https://doi.org/10.1002/ejsp.674

LeDoux, J. E. (1996). *The emotional brain: The mysterious underpinnings of emotional life.* Simon & Schuster.

Lieberman, M. D., Eisenberger, N. I., Crockett, M. J., Tom, S. M., Pfeifer, J. H., & Way, B. M. (2007). Putting feelings into words: Affect labeling disrupts amygdala activity in response to affective stimuli. *Psychological Science, 18*(5), 421–428. https://doi.org/10.1111/j.1467-9280.2007.01916.x

Linehan, M. M. (1993). *Cognitive-behavioral treatment of borderline personality disorder.* Guilford Press.

Milton, D. E. M. (2012). On the ontological status of autism: The 'double empathy problem'. *Disability & Society, 27*(6), 883–887. https://doi.org/10.1080/09687599.2012.710008

Neff, K. D. (2003). Self-compassion: An alternative conceptualization of a healthy attitude toward oneself. *Self and Identity, 2*(2), 85–101. https://doi.org/10.1080/15298868.2003.9683032

Porges, S. W. (2011). *The polyvagal theory: Neurophysiological foundations of emotions, attachment, communication, and self-regulation.* W. W. Norton & Company.

Price, D. (2022). *Unmasking autism: Discovering the new faces of neurodiversity.* Harmony Books.

Sapolsky, R. M. (2017). *Behave: The biology of humans at our best and worst.* Penguin Press.

Siegel, D. J. (2012). *The developing mind: How relationships and the brain interact to shape who we are* (2nd ed.). Guilford Press.

van der Kolk, B. A. (2014). *The body keeps the score: Brain, mind, and body in the healing of trauma.* Viking.

Acknowledgments

Writing this book was not a straight line. It was a collection of pivots, scraped knees, late-night doubts, unexpected clarity, and more deep breaths than I care to admit. I wouldn't be here without the people who held me together, nudged me forward, or simply reminded me I wasn't crazy for wanting more out of my life.

To Bryan, my steady place to land. Thank you for loving me in every version of myself, even the exhausted, unraveling, rebuilding ones. Thank you for giving me room to reach for things that scared me and cheering even when the process was messy. You made this possible in a hundred quiet ways.

To Collin and Brynn, who are proof that perspective shifts are not just tools but lifelines. You teach me every day why emotional intelligence matters and why breaking generational patterns is worth the discomfort. Watching you grow into who you are becoming is one of my greatest joys.

To my mom, who taught me resilience through every storm. And to my dad, who showed me that quitting was never an option, even when things got hard. The foundation of my strength starts with both of you.

To my sister-in-law, Tessa, who was my first reader and truth-teller. Your perspective helped me clarify my message when I was still finding the words. Thank you for your patience, heart, and the questions that pushed me to go deeper.

To Kat Klumpp, my ride-or-die sounding board through this entire journey.

You stayed with me through every pivot, every new idea that popped into my head, and every moment I doubted myself. Your unwavering presence and honest feedback kept me grounded when my thoughts spiraled out of control. This book exists because you believed in it—and in me—even when I couldn't see it clearly myself.

To my WEG family. You sharpened my voice, trusted my expertise, and let me show up as the advocate, strategist, and leader I was built to be. Every student, every parent, every case, every late-night crisis call shaped the clarity behind this book. You taught me how powerful it is when people are truly seen.

To Holly Christensen Sestak, CEO and President of Socratic Arts. You took a chance on me during a career transition and opened a door when I needed it most. That opportunity became a turning point, and the ripple of that choice still moves through everything I do.

To Wes Bergmann and The Blox family, who reawakened the entrepreneurial fire in me—and brought my confidence back to life. The Perspective Pivot was born from the energy, grit, and unfiltered truth of those rooms. Being surrounded by people building their dreams cracked something open in me that I had long buried under burnout. Wes, you didn't just endorse this book—you've challenged me to show up and do the work, even when it's uncomfortable, even when I doubt myself. That steady push forward has been a gift I didn't know I needed.

To Andrea Holmes Thompkins, who saw the whole package in me before I fully saw it in myself. From the moment we met through The Blox, you've been one of the first to say 'yes' to my vision and to believe that the world will need to look out when I step fully into my power. Your belief in me has been a catalyst, and I'm grateful for your fierce support and the doors you've helped me see I'm capable of walking through.

To the clients, families, emerging adults, and beautifully complex minds who have trusted me with their stories. You showed me the patterns behind the struggle, the neuroscience beneath the overwhelm, and the resilience inside every brain. This work exists because of you.

To the researchers, scientists, and educators whose work gave me the language for what I was seeing in my clients and in myself. Dr. Lisa Feldman Barrett, Dr. Dan Siegel, Dr. Bruce Perry—your decades of research laid the foundation for the science in these pages. You helped me transform instinct into evidence.

And to you, the reader. Thank you for choosing to explore your own mind with honesty, courage, and curiosity. Thank you for being willing to pivot, even when it feels uncomfortable. My hope is that this book helps you reclaim clarity, confidence, and compassion for yourself. If it does, every hard moment that went into writing it was worth it.

Thank you for walking this part of the journey with me.

About the Author

Dr. Kristen C. Eccleston is a Brain Processing & Neurodivergent Expert, TEDx speaker, and national entrepreneurship competition winner, with an Ed.D. in Mind, Brain, and Teaching from Johns Hopkins University. For 20 years she has done one thing: get to the root of what keeps complex brains stuck — and help people see the way they think and learn not as a limitation, but as a gift. She created The Perspective Pivot from that work to do one thing: give people the science behind why their brain spirals, and the tools to stop letting it run their life.

A NOTE FROM DR. KRISTEN

If you've made it this far, something in these pages resonated with you. Maybe you recognized yourself in the spirals. Maybe you tried the Triple-A Hand Hack and felt something shift. Maybe you're still skeptical but curious enough to keep going.

Whatever brought you here, I want you to know this: the work doesn't stop when you close this book. The Perspective Pivot isn't a one-time fix—it's a practice, a skill that gets stronger the more you use it.

I've created a resource hub with tools to help you integrate this work into your daily life. You'll find practice trackers, reflection prompts, and other materials I use with my private clients—the things that didn't fit in these pages but will help you keep the momentum going.

Access your reader resources here:

drkristeneccleston.com/the-perspective-pivot

And I genuinely want to hear from you. Share your pivots, your questions, your breakthroughs, or the moments when your brain tried to convince you this wouldn't work for you.

FOR ORGANIZATIONS, EDUCATORS, AND EVENT PLANNERS

Interested in bringing The Perspective Pivot to your team, organization, or event? Bulk copies are available for conferences, corporate training, healthcare teams, schools, and professional development programs. To inquire about bulk orders, keynote bookings, or workshop facilitation, visit drkristeneccleston.com

You can connect with me on:

https://drkristeneccleston.com

https://www.facebook.com/kristeneccleston

https://www.linkedin.com/in/kristen-eccleston-the-neurodiverse-teacher-keynote-speaker

https://www.instagram.com/dr.kristen.e

https://www.tiktok.com/@dr.kristen_e